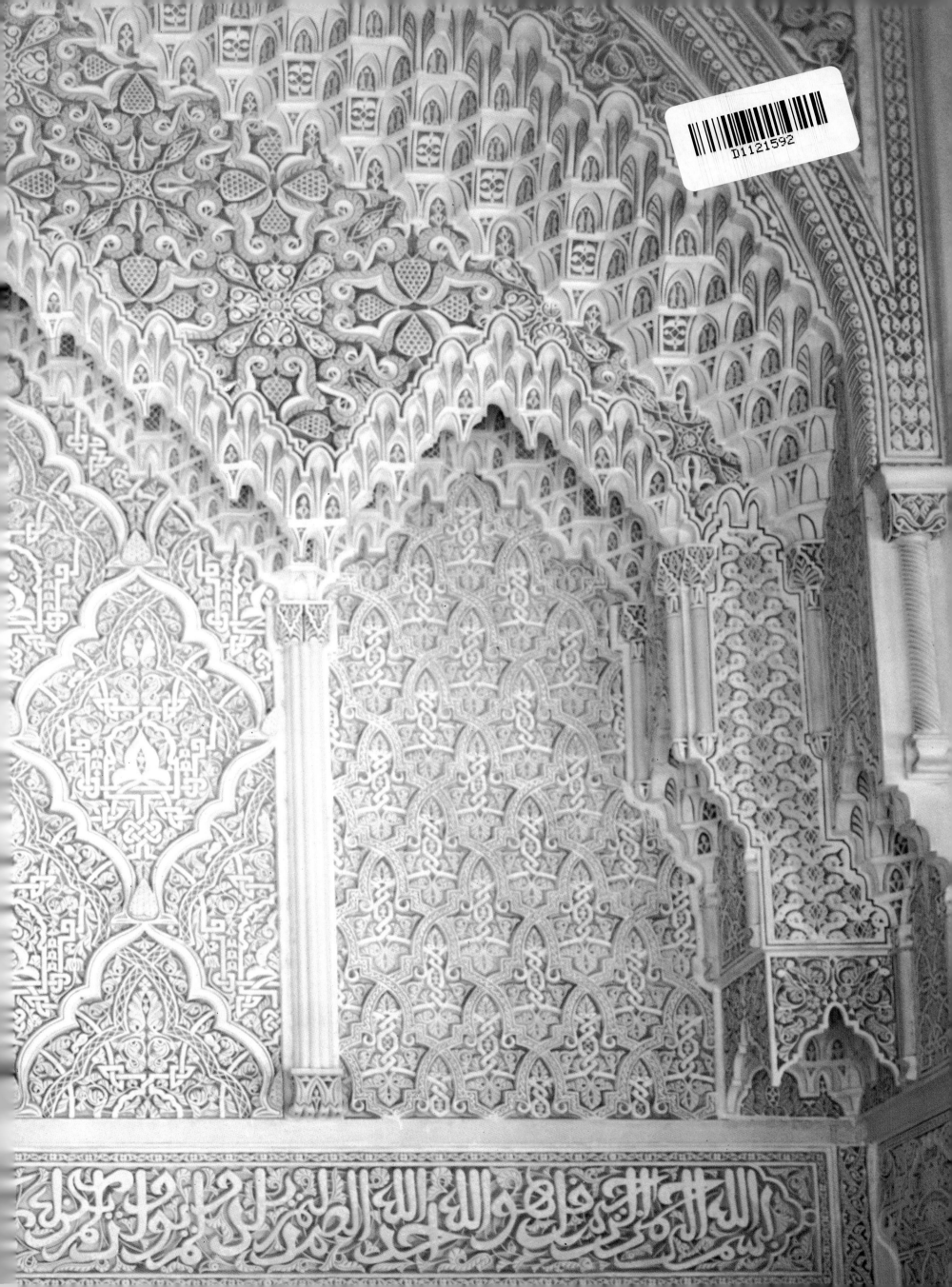

AFRICA
THE MIGHTY CONTINENT

RUPERT O. MATTHEWS

THE IMAGE BANK

ISBN 0-941267-07-5

For rights information about the photographs in
this book please contact:

The Image Bank
111 Fifth Avenue, New York, NY 10003

Manufactured in Spain

Producer: Ted Smart
Author: Rupert O. Matthews
Design: Sara Cooper
Photo Research: Tamara Kahn/Edward Douglas
Production Assistant: Seni Glaister
Illustration courtesy of Bernard Thornton Artists

AFRICA

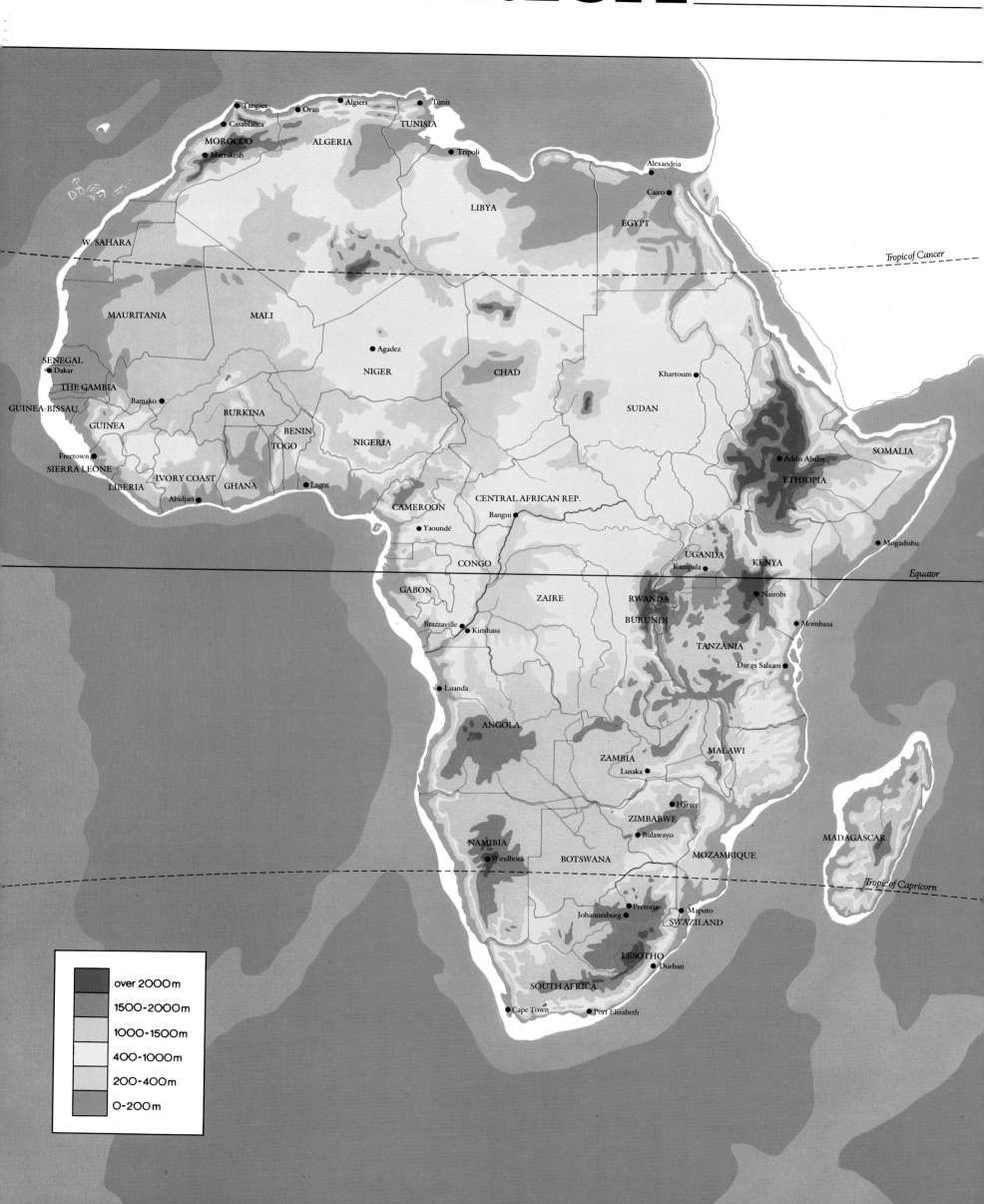

Tangier •   • Oran   • Algiers   • Tunis

Casablanca •

TUNISIA

MOROCCO

ALGERIA

Marrakesh •

• Tripoli

Alexandria •

LIBYA

EGYPT

Cairo •

Tropic of Cancer

W. SAHARA

MAURITANIA

MALI

NIGER

CHAD

SUDAN

Agadez •

Khartoum •

SENEGAL

Dakar •

THE GAMBIA

Bamako •

BURKINA

GUINEA-BISSAU

GUINEA

BENIN

TOGO

NIGERIA

CENTRAL AFRICAN REP.

Addis Ababa •

SOMALIA

Freetown •

SIERRA LEONE

IVORY COAST

GHANA

ETHIOPIA

LIBERIA

Abidjan •

Lagos •

CAMEROON

Bangui •

Yaoundé •

Mogadishu •

CONGO

UGANDA

KENYA

GABON

Kampala •

ZAIRE

Nairobi •

RWANDA

Equator

Brazzaville •

• Kinshasa

BURUNDI

Mombasa •

TANZANIA

Dar es Salaam •

Luanda •

ANGOLA

ZAMBIA

MALAWI

Lusaka •

Harare •

ZIMBABWE

MADAGASCAR

Bulawayo •

NAMIBIA

MOZAMBIQUE

Windhoek •

BOTSWANA

Tropic of Capricorn

Pretoria •

Maputo •

Johannesburg •

SWAZILAND

LESOTHO

Durban •

SOUTH AFRICA

Cape Town •

• Port Elizabeth

over 2000m

1500-2000m

1000-1500m

400-1000m

200-400m

0-200m

They used to call it the Dark Continent. A vast empty space on the maps of the world filled in only by the vague tales of tribesmen and the fever-ridden dreams of explorers. It was a land where almost anything could be believed, and almost anything could happen.

Today the wonders of technology, satellites and the like, have filled in many of the blanks. The mountains have been mapped and the rivers navigated. But the mystery remains. The mystery of trackless deserts untrodden by humans and of endless forests.

Nowhere is the sense of mystery stronger than in Egypt, the land of lost cities and bustling markets. Where everywhere can be seen the work of the long dead hands of the pharaohs and the influence of the Nile.

It was the Nile which created Egypt and without the great river the nation could not exist today. It is the river which brings life to the burning desert. The broad floodplain which spreads out on either side of the river is rich and fertile, producing huge crops of grain, cotton and dates. But beyond the plain is the barren desert, devoid of life where temperatures can soar to unbearable heights during the day and then plummet at night. Often the divide between the fertile and the desolate is sudden and marked. It is possible to stand with one foot on richly growing crops, and the other on shifting sand.

Only the complex irrigation system maintains the farmland. Water is drawn from the Nile, often by traditional hand-operated shadufs, levered buckets operated by rope. From the river a network of channels, both large and small, carries the water to the thirsty crops. It is a system which has been the basis of Egyptian life for thousands of years, right back to the days of the pharaohs, and beyond.

It was some time around 3,000 BC that Menes, king of the Nile Valley as far south as modern Aswan, conquered the fertile Delta and became the first Pharaoh, the god-king of all Egypt. For the first time the vast resources of the rich Nile lands were united under the control of a single ruler. At once the benefits began to be felt.

New irrigation projects were undertaken, in one instance the entire river was diverted, and a new capital city was built. This was Memphis, just south of modern Cairo, destined to become one of the greatest cities of ancient Egypt. There is little left of Memphis today, centuries of neglect and flooding have destroyed the great palaces and temples of Menes.

But the burial grounds of the city rank amongst the greatest sights in the world. These are the great pyramids which dominate both the landscape and the public imagination.

The oldest pyramid was that of Pharaoh Zoser at Saqqara, built around 2650 BC. To the ancient Egyptians their pharaoh was a living god and his death was merely his passing from this world to another. His spirit demanded a home and all the goods he used in life. It was this belief which led to the construction of the massive monuments to the dead king and the complex of temples and rooms around his burial.

At Saqqara the pyramid proper was surrounded by acres of land devoted to temples and storehouses, all for the use of the dead

Facing page: The Pyramid of Chephron rises above the Sphinx at Giza. The Pyramid of Chephron is the only one of the three great pyramids to retain some of its original granite casing, that of the others having been looted to build Cairo. Above: A wall painting from the tomb of a nobleman in the Valley of the Kings, near Luxor. The scene shows the produce of the nobleman's estates being presented to him by servants. Such pictures are common in Egyptian tombs, it being hoped that the opulence so depicted would continue in the afterlife. Left: A statue of an unidentified queen. Below: The massive statues of Rameses II at Abu Simbel. Their true bulk can only be appreciated from close quarters.

Zoser. Dozens of other tombs and small pyramids, belonging to courtiers and other pharaohs, cluster around.

But it is a few miles away at Giza that the pyramid builders surpassed themselves. Here that the three great pyramids stand. The pyramid of Cheops is the largest standing 450 feet high and covering some 13 acres of ground. It has been estimated that this solid mass of masonry contains two and a half million blocks of stone, each weighing over two tons. Its construction was a stupendous undertaking for a civilisation which had not yet mastered the use of iron. It is thought that the pyramid was built over a period of perhaps twenty years by hundreds of

thousands of farmers who were seasonally idle due to the timing of the agricultural year.

Within the Great Pyramid was buried the Pharaoh Cheops. Today his burial chamber can be entered through an entrance 55 feet above the ground which leads into a magnificent stone gallery 150 feet long and 30 feet high. The burial chamber itself is 34 feet by 17 and contains nothing but an empty sarcophagus. It is assumed by most archaeologists that the tomb was robbed of its treasures in antiquity. Some, however, believe that the ancients may have been more cunning than has been thought and that Cheops still rests with his treasure in some secret chamber as yet unfound.

The two remaining great pyramids were built by Cheops' son, Chephren, and his grandson, Mycerinus. They are smaller than that of Cheops, standing 400 feet and 200 feet tall respectively. All three were built with quite amazing skill. The massive blocks of limestone are fitted together so exactly that it is impossible to insert a knifeblade between them.

Slightly southeast of the pyramids stands the famous Sphinx. The statue was carved from a ridge of limestone and stands over 60 feet tall and 200 feet long. It was carved by Chephren to face the rising sun in honour of Horus, the Sun God.

About 400 years after the building of the pyramids Egypt collapsed into civil war and upheaval. After generations of conflict a new unified state grew up centered on Thebes, modern Luxor, far to the south. It is here that the greatest wealth of ancient Egyptian monuments are centered.

The massive Karnak Temple is the largest and best preserved temple in Egypt. Indeed it is the largest temple anywhere in the world. Dedicated to the sun god Amon-Ra, the temple dates back to around 1900 BC. It is made up of massive pillared halls and huge pylon gateways where nearly every surface is covered in hieroglyphics recording the deeds of kings and gods.

Within the temple complex lies the Hypostyle Hall containing no less than 134 columns, the central rows being 69 feet tall and

33 feet around. The sheer scale of the Hall is overwhelming to the visitor and has ensured that the site is featured in numerous films and travelogues.

A short distance across the river and into the desert is the famous Valley of the Kings. It was here that the Theban pharaohs constructed their tombs and funeral temples. The tombs were excavated from the rocky walls of the valley in an attempt to frustrate tomb robbers. Only one pharaoh managed to escape the robbers, at least until the 20th century archaeologists arrived.

This was Tutankhamun, a fairly unimportant pharaoh who died when still in his teens. His tomb is now open to the public and contains some fine wall paintings and carvings. The rich contents of the tomb, including the magnificent gold mask are in a museum in Cairo. More than 60 royal tombs lie in the valley, together with many belonging to the nobility.

Close by the tombs stand the two collosi of Memnon, a pair of 60 feet tall seated statues of Amenhotep III. They were erected about 1500 BC and for many years one of them emitted an eerie singing sound as the rising sun struck its face. No convincing explanation for this has ever been given.

Some miles upstream of Luxor is the architectural masterpiece of the great warrior-pharaoh Rameses II. The temple of Abu Simbel has now been moved several hundred feet uphill to escape the waters of Lake Nassar, created by the Aswan High Dam. It was cut into the solid rock of a cliff face about 3,200 years ago and extends more than 200 feet. Flanking the entrance are four huge seated statues of Rameses himself, each more than 60 feet tall. Smaller statues of the royal family and gods accompany the god-king.

Within the temple are three dark halls containing pillars and statues together with wall paintings and carvings of exquisite

Egypt is a land dominated by the past. The great pyramids and the Sphinx tower over the desert at Giza, west of Cairo and are the subject of a spectacular son et lumiere show each evening. Treasures recovered from tombs, those (below and facing page) are from the tomb of Tutankhamun, reveal much about the everyday life of the pharaohs. Overleaf: The spectacular entrance to the temple at Abu Simbel.

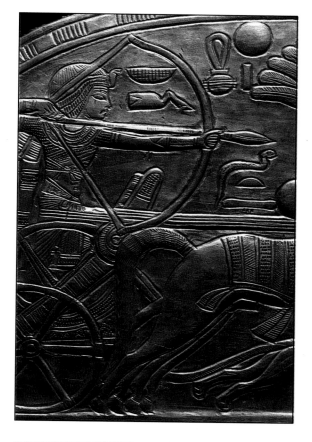

beauty. Deep within the temple lies the small chamber containing the statues of the sun gods Ra and Amun and the underworld god Ptah. On two days of the year the rising sun penetrates the entire length of the temple to illuminate the sacred statues.

It is at Abu Simbel that the contrasts of Egypt come face to face. The great statues of the pharaoh gaze out across a lake which did not exist when the temple was built. Lake Nassar was created in 1971 when the Aswan High Dam was completed.

This massive engineering project was built largely by the Russians, using Egyptian labour. The completed dam is over two miles long and 360 feet high, stretching right across the Nile Valley. The dam made it possible to control the annual flood waters of the Nile and to produce massive amounts of electricity from the river.

Unfortunately it also had the effect of stopping the annual deposit of fertile silts on the fields of the lower valley. Since before the time of the pharaohs Egyptian farmers relied on this silt as the basis for their agriculture. Now they have to spend money on artificial fertilizers. There is much debate as to whether or not the advantages of the dam outweigh its disadvantages, whether it would have been better not to have built it at all.

Between the ancient world of pharaohs and the modern face of the Aswan dam stretch many hundreds of years, years which have created the Egypt which the visitor sees today. It is basically a country where the Islam of the invading Arabs has been grafted on to the older culture of the pharaohs.

The Nile below Aswan High Dam is a fine example of all that is traditional in Egypt. The blue waters of the Nile are dotted by the

triangular white sails of the fellucas, the traditional river craft of Egypt. The battered, sunburnt wood of the hull and mast contrasts sharply with the sails, almost blindingly white in the noon sun and the dark waters of the Nile.

These river craft are ideally suited to the Nile. Their shallow draughts enable them to run across the numerous sandbanks of the river while their peculiar rig allows their crew to take advantage of the desert wind, no matter in which direction it blows. At Aswan the fellucas operate as ferries, carrying passengers from the city across the river or to any of the many islands which dot the river here. Elsewhere the picturesque boats con-

Temples were among the most important buildings in ancient Egypt. Luxor Temple (below) was dedicated to the state god Amun, one of the three gods celebrated at Abu Simbel (bottom), the other two being Path and Harakte. The great statues which flank temple entrances are not of the gods, but of the pharaohs who built the temples, in both these cases Rameses II. The huge statues (facing page), near Aswan, are of Amenophis III, an earlier pharaoh, though the temple they once flanked has long since vanished. Right: Heiroglyphics at the Komombo Temple. Overleaf: The tomb of the Aga Khan on the east bank of the Nile at Aswan.

but the larger structures have a magnificence which dwarfs all other religious structures. In Cairo, once the cultural heart of Islam, stand some of the finest mosques to be seen anywhere in the world.

The modern city of Cairo was founded by the Fatimid general Jawhar al-Saqally in 969 to replace the earlier Heliopolis which dated back to the pharaohs. Heliopolis had been founded as a cult center for the worship of the sun-god. To emphasize the Islamic nature of his creation Jawhar al-Saqally began the Al Azhar mosque as his first major building. It is a beautiful creation.

The Al Azhar was established as a center

tinue their age-old business of transporting crops from farms to market, a sign of the unchanging face of this ancient land, even in the bustling 20th century.

The streets of Aswan, too, present a traditional face. It is a scene repeated in many towns down along the Nile - Qena, Asyut, El Minya, Beni Suef and Idfu - but at Aswan the tiny network of crowded, narrow streets, packed with tradesmen and dealers has a charm all its own. There are the copperware shops where the smith sits amongst his products on the roadside and the cloth sellers with their bales of brightly coloured cotton and thick felts. The cafes are as richly oriental as any throughout the Middle East and offer a variety of dishes. The tilapia fish caught in the Nile is a tempting local delicacy, but lamb kebabs and bean dishes are almost ubiquitous through Egypt.

The dominating influence is that of Islam, which overran Egypt in 640. At first only the invading Arabs practiced Islam, the mass of the people clinging to Christianity or even the older pagan beliefs. With time, however, the native population became converted and now every town and village has its mosque. The smaller mosques, in villages and city quarters have a simple charm, though a non-believing visitor is not always welcome,

In many ways Egypt is timeless. The mosaic (above) depicts the age of the pharaohs, yet its fish, dogs and loinclothed men have their modern counterparts. The fellah climbing the mast of his felucca (above left) is only the most recent of hundreds of generations of his predecessors who have made a living by transporting people and goods on the Nile. The impressive mausoleum (left) was built for the Aga Khan, who died in 1957, continuing the old tradition of impressive Egyptian tombs.

for the study of the Koran and has remained so to this day. The early scripture classes have now expanded to form a university with some 20,000 students studying a variety of subjects. But the heart of the complex, now adorned with a modern library and lecture halls, remains the mosque. The large building is dominated by the dome, covered with patterned tiles, and the twin cupolas of the square minaret.

Clustering around Al Azhar are a collection of mosques whose spindly minarets give this area of the city the feeling of being a tranquil forest of stone. The cry of muezzin at prayer time is inescapable and forms the characteristic sound of Cairo.

The holiest of these mosques is the Al Hussein where many relics are kept and which is a focus for the devout. Christians and other non-Muslims are forbidden to enter this holiest of Egyptian buildings. The nearby Sultan Hassan mosque is a lavish example of medieval Islamic architecture from a time when Cairo was at the height of its power and wealth. Its minaret, at 250 feet is the second highest on the continent.

Cairo has its secular side as well and the spreading bazaar is one of the largest in Africa. There are streets specialising in particular goods, be they clothing, jewellery, reproduction pharaonic trinkets, leather goods or almost anything else. It is here that the ordinary Cairene does his buying and here that the best bargains are to be had. The air is filled with the constant chatter of bargaining. No good having a set price, it is

Great changes came to Egypt following the Macedonian invasion of 332BC. At a desert temple, (above) the Temple at Hathor at Derdera, the Macedonian king Alexander the Great was proclaimed an Egyptian god. He went on to found the port city of Alexandria, where the Muntazah Palace (left) stands. The palace was built by the Khedive Abbas in 1892. Below: A felucca on the Upper Nile.

up to the customer and the stallholder to agree a suitable rate. The pretend disinterest of the potential buyer and over-enthusiastic praising of the seller can make the bazaar a fascinating place, even for those not interested in buying anything.

Cairo stands at the southern end of the great delta, forming a link between the fertile lands and the historic past of the upper valley. In the northwest, at the coastal fringe of the delta stands Alexandria, a city which links Egypt with the Mediterranean world.

Alexandria was founded by the Macedonian king Alexander the Great in 332 after conquering Egypt in a lightning campaign. He left after only a few months, entrusting the newly acquired lands to his general Ptolemy, who later made himself pharaoh of an independent Egypt.

Ptolemy made Alexandria into a Greek city on the fringes of the ancient heritage of Egypt. In many ways the city has never been assimilated into Egyptian culture, and retains its own style. The waterfront is dominated by soaring hotels and office blocks, the sandy coves around the city are given over to bathing beaches and the whole city has a definite Mediterranean feel which would not be out of place in Greece or southern Italy. Only in the bazaars of the city center can a hint of Upper Egypt be found.

Most of the glories of Alexandria are gone. Most recently the annual court visits paid by the Kings of Egypt through most of the 19th century have ceased. Further back in time the magnificent Library, containing the greatest collection of books in the world and, reputedly, the entire written history of Egypt to pre-Pharaonic days, was burnt by the rampaging Roman legionnaries of Julius Caesar. Even the famous lighthouse, one of the Seven Wonders of the World, has gone. The huge tower stood about 300 feet tall and sent out a light visible for more than 30 miles out to sea which guided the grains ships into port. The tower was begun in 297 BC and may have been completed fifteen years later. It was destroyed by an earthquake in 1303.

Above: One of the many rock-cut temples of Upper Egypt. The only light to enter these cavernous structures enters by the narrow doorway. Right: The rough surface of the Great Pyramid becomes clear at close quarters. The limestone blocks are about three feet deep and weigh several tons each. It is thought that they were placed in position by gangs of workmen with the aid of rollers and levers. Far right: The traditional veil of the desert nomad.

The city once held the tomb of Alexander the Great, the founder of the city and the largest empire the world had yet seen. That too has disappeared.

But if so much of Alexandria has vanished it is because the city itself has remained so vibrant and important. The city was created to be a major port and has continued to fulfil

that function ever since. The constant demand for space and new buildings has led to the replacement of the ancient city with the new.

It is at the long abandoned sites such as Karnak and Giza that the magnificent heritage of Egypt can still be seen. It is ironic that so many of these monuments are to be found

in the desert. To the ancient Egyptians the desert was a hostile and dangerous place, the land of the dead. That desert spreads out from the limits of the Nile floodplain to both south and west for many thousands of miles.

To the south lie the two desert states of Chad and Sudan. The size of the desert is truly vast, covering more land than most of

the world's countries, and stretching to endless horizons devoid of life. At various places oases and rough grazing provide enough food for the herds of the desert tribes. For centuries the nomads supplemented their meager resources by periodic raids into more settled lands.

It was in this way that the Tuareg, Toubou and other tribes became superb horsemen and greatly feared fighters. The culture built up by the proud, warlike tribes was remarkable. It was dominated by a fierce Islamic faith and by an honor which demanded swift retribution for any insult.

For centuries the tough desert fighters dominated not only the desert but the lands around. The coming of colonialism curbed their power, but the area is now plunged into bitter fighting as the desert peoples attempt to regain their accustomed dominance.

Though largely desert, both Chad and Sudan have fertile, watered areas. The southern areas of Chad are watered by frequent rains which support large grazing herds and some crops. But the most noticeable feature of the area is Lake Chad, the 11th largest lake in the world.

To find a lake covering some 8,000 square miles in a near desert region is remarkable, and Lake Chad is like no other on earth. It lies at the heart of a great depression, covering parts of seven nations, and has no outlet to the sea.

Above left, above right and top right: Camels and horses are shown to tourists at the great pyramids of Giza. Below: Animal-headed gods in a tomb painting in the Valley of the Kings. It is thought that pre-dynastic Egyptians worshipped animal gods,

these were later anthropomorphized to create the later gods. The gods generally retained some of their animalistic attributes. Anubis, the jackal god, being the god of the dead because of that animal's scavenging habits.

It is dependent on the irregular rainfall of the region for its very existence. After years of drought it may shrink to cover just 4,000 square miles while a heavy deluge will swell it to some 10,000 square miles.

In times of flood the great stands of papyrus reeds and other water plants will float free of the loose sandy bed. They drift

around the surface of the lake until the waters fall and they can take root once more.

Sudan finds its water source, like Egypt, in the Nile. But in Sudan the Nile is a very different river, indeed it is three rivers. It is at the great city of Khartoum that the three come together.

From the south comes the stately White Nile, from its headwaters deep in tropical Africa. Tumbling down from the southeast is the more turbulent Blue Nile which finds its origins in the mountains of Ethiopia. The two great rivers come together to form a third, the Nile which flows northward through the Sudan to Egypt and the Mediterranean.

It is the joining of the two tributaries which gives the lower Nile its special character. The White Nile is a large river throughout the year, drawing on the steady rains of the interior. It is this which provides the lower Nile with the bulk of its water. The Blue Nile is a shallow stream for most of the year, but changes to a raging torrent after the summer rains in Ethiopia. The massive surge plunges on down the Nile to create the annual floods which brought fertile silt to the fields of Egypt. The floods have now been contained by the Aswan High Dam.

It is not only the great rivers which join at Khartoum, but also the cultures of the region. The north of Sudan is almost entirely desert, frequented only by a few desert

nomads. The south is a land of forest, swamp and high rainfall. Around Khartoum itself the land is scrubby and experiences seasonal summer rainfall.

The population of Khartoum and the surrounding lands is Arabic, as is the culture of the city. The minarets of mosques dominate the skyline and the cry of the muezzins fills the air at prayertime.

It would be wrong to think of Khartoum as an ancient city, despite its dusty, timeless face. It was founded in the 1820s, but completely destroyed during the uprising led by the religious leader known as the Mahdi in 1885. The modern town dates from the 1890s.

Khartoum is the financial center of Sudan, but the cultural heart lies in Omdurman, just across the White Nile. The city had its origins in the camp set up by the Mahdi when his forces were besieging Khartoum in 1885. In the final assault Khartoum was destroyed and its British/Egyptian garrison slaughtered.

The most startling building in Omdurman, the Mahdi's Tomb, dates back only to 1947. Its five glittering silver domes and tranquil park were erected by the Mahdi's son after the original tomb was destroyed by the British in 1897. The building is considered sacred and only true believers of the Mahdi are allowed to enter.

The unique Sudanese form of Islam can also be seen in the graveyard on the outskirts of Omdurman on Friday afternoons. After attending prayers and a sermon in the mosques, the members of the Tariqa sect gather at the graveyard to perform their mystic whirling dance.

These are the whirling dervishes who spin incessantly on one spot to whirl themselves into a trance-like condition. The more fervent dancers may fall into twitching convulsions or simply collapse. Several hundred people may gather regularly to take part in this peculiarly Sudanese ritual.

Far to the east lies the city of Kassala, once

the main trade route to Ethiopia, is possibly the most beautiful city in the Sudan. The city proper is surrounded by vast orchards of tangerine, banana and guava trees. Within the city the magnificent market and the colorful tribesmen who trade there.

Providing a romantic backdrop to Kassala are the two magnificent jebels, hills carved to a sugar-loaf shape by constant desert erosion. The larger of the two hills, Taka, has at its summit a tree the leaves of which are said to be magical, for those brave enough to risk the climb.

East of Kassala lies Ethiopia, an anomaly amongst African nations. Apart from a brief occupation by Italy, Ethiopia has never been colonized by a European power. Its history dates right back to the 3rd century BC, when the pharaohs still ruled in Egypt. In the 4th century AD the nation became converted to Christianity and established an empire which persisted until Moslem attacks disrupted Ethiopia in the 17th century. The empire was

reformed a century later, only to be overthrown by a military coup in the 1960s which called on Russia for aid.

Today, Ethiopia is a strange amalgam of medieval feudalism, military power and communist ideals. It is also a nation plunged into civil war as various constituent peoples try to break away.

The country itself is a magnificent panorama of mountains, lakes and valleys. It is in the heights of the plateau that the Blue Nile has its source and from these mountains that it draws the flood waters which surge downstream to run against the Aswan High Dam.

The traditional culture of the Ethiopians is perhaps best expressed in the curious ritual of the armed charge. Mounted warriors of the desert tribes execute a ragged charge towards spectators which ends in a dramatic volley of musket fire. It was these proud, savage warriors who faced the tanks and guns of the Italians in the 1930s. And the same people who took control of the uprising which

Previous pages: The gleaming waters of Lake Chad. Far left: The Nile at Khartoum, capital of the Sudan. Left: The minaret of the Grand Mosque of Khartoum which, despite appearances, is of 20th century construction. Below: The strange jebel hills of Kassala, only one of which has ever been climbed.

overthrew the Emperor Haile Salasie.

In recent years the mountains of southeastern Ethiopia have revealed one of the most magnificent caves in the world. Stretching more than 9 miles through the hills, the Sof Omar Cave has been carved by a river with cuts a broad, looping path through the rocks.

The capital of Addis Ababa is one of the few areas still open to foreigners. It consists of a sprawling urban area which shows clear signs of the Italian occupation and present Russian influence. Broadly speaking, however, Ethiopia has remained free of foreign pressure. Its food, for example, remains a

blend of sour millet bread, fiery lentil brews and rather dubious salads. Only in the larger towns is a more varied diet and culture available.

Far to the northwest, across the vast stretches of the Sahara, a broadly similar nomadic culture dominates Libya. This desert nation is fiercely Islamic and dominated by centuries of nomadic pastoralism. In recent years some attempts at introducing agriculture have been made, but it is oil which is the basis of the wealth of the nation.

Vast amounts of oil are produced each year to support the economy, yet it is the desert which remains the dominating factor in Libyan life. The culture of the Arabian tribes is to be seen everywhere and few signs in a language other than Arabic can be found.

The rural population find their living traditionally from the herding of sheep and goats across the vast stretches of poor grazing and scattered oases of the southern deserts. The nomadic life of these people is almost archetypically Arabian, with the use of camels and horses for transport and felt tents for homes. At regular intervals the nomads gather at oasis villages for the markets where they sell their animals in exchange for various goods.

Along the fertile coastal strip of the country can be found a number of magnificent ancient ruins. Perhaps the finest are those at Leptis Magna where an extensive Roman city was abandoned and has been preserved by the hot desert air. In Roman times the

Despite the fact that it is a desert country, much of the Sudan can be made fertile by irrigation. Straw (above) is a valued commodity, being used for thatching (left), basketry and other purposes. Below: The *Nile at Omdurman. Overleaf: A desert village near Kassala.*

Libyan coast was a fertile region which provided grain for much of the empire. Many years of overcultivation and changing climate have conspired to strip much of the land of its fertility.

To the west, Algeria is a land divided into two dramatically separate parts. Along the coast is a land of vineyards and wheat fields.

It is along this strip that the majority of the population lives, and always has done so. Roman ruins can be found in plenty here, among them some of the most important in the whole Mediterranean. Those at Tipasa are perhaps the most popular with visitors. Throughout the days of the Roman Empire this region remained crucially important due

to its fertility and grain production.

Clinging to the rocky coast are many fishing villages and harbors of which the greatest is Algiers itself. The city has been a port for over 4,000 years, though its population has only been large for the past five centuries. It is a magnificent jewel of North African culture, epitomising much that is

Ethiopia (these pages) is a land of contrasts. It has soaring desert mountains and fertile lowland plains. Unlike other North African nations, Ethiopia maintained its Christianity throughout *the Islamic conquests of a thousand years ago. Its recent history has been dominated by revolution, civil war and famine, all of which have hindered the economic development of the nation.*

The ruins of Leptis Magna (above) in Libya are a magnificent reminder of the ancient civilisation which flourished along the North African coast. The city dates back to the 5th century BC, when it was a Phoenician settlement, and was conquered by Rome in 146BC. It later became a major city, one of its sons becoming the Roman Emperor Septimus Severus. Since the destruction of Roman civilisation in the area by invading Vandals, the lands have belonged to the desert Tuaregs. These proud people are expert horsemen and camelriders with a fierce Islamic faith. In the past thirty years oil, (bottom right) a refinery, has become the dominant economic force. Overleaf: The sands of the Sahara.

unique about the life of the region.

The hill which forms the center of the city is crowned by the ruined fortress of the Fort of the Kasbah, once the stronghold of the pirate chieftains who ruled the town and preyed on shipping throughout the western Mediterranean.

Below the fortress is the Kasbah proper, a dense area of traditional Algerian culture. The narrow streets of this old quarter form a labyrinth of twisting passages, stairways and overhanging balconies. It is to many the epitome of an Arabian shopping center of the traditional type, with small shops and bustling traders.

At the foot of the slope on which the Kasbah stands is the large Place des Martyrs which is dominated by two fine mosques. El Kebir dates back over 900 years and is one of the finest in the country. North of the square and the Kasbah are the broad boulevards built by the French during their long occupation of Algeria.

All along the coast lies a string of smaller towns and villages with a similar division between French and Arab quarters. Of these perhaps the most delightful is Oran, which lies in a spectacularly scenic bay. The elegant French buildings of the seafront are backed by the tangled maze of narrow streets which makes up Old Oran.

East of the towns of Algeria the coast drops down to form level plains and low hills. It is here that the modern city of Tunis dominates the country of Tunisia. Like so many other cities of North Africa, Tunis has two centers and two very different atmospheres.

To the east, bordering the Lake of Tunis is the elegant, boulevarded city built by the French last century. Broad avenues, lined with eucalyptus and palm trees run along a regular grid and meet at wide, magnificent squares.

To the west is the Mediana, the old quarter. It is here that the true Arab culture of Tunis comes to the fore. Small shops, crowded together in narrow streets sell a variety of goods, including fine carpets and metalwork. Like all North African trading centers, the Medina is filled by the scents of spice and crowded humanity and the sounds of bargaining and argument.

But the Medina contains not only crowded shopping streets. There are long narrow streets faced by tall, blank walls. Only the occasional massive wooden door, studded with nails and borne on huge hinges, reveals that these are the most opulent streets in the old quarter. The traditional form of a luxurious town house in Tunis is that of a large house centered around an open courtyard. All rooms and corridors open off the courtyard, or courtyards. Only a solid, drab wall is presented to the street.

Within, the house may be a jewel of luxury, with marbled floors, columned halls and playing fountains. As an anti-burglar measure in the midst of a crowded city the drab, high exterior walls can only be admired.

At the heart of the Medina stands the Great Mosque, begun back in 732. The scholars of Tunis were once famous for their learning, dominating the intellectual life of Islam. Today their theological reputation has been overtaken by others, but the magnificent mosque remains.

A few miles to the north of Tunis lie the ruins of Carthage. It was this city which was the only ancient power able seriously to threaten the rise of the Roman Empire. In a devastating series of wars spread over more than a century Carthage was destroyed, finally falling in 146 BC. Very little of this old city remains, the ruins visible today dating mainly to the Roman period.

But the finest ruins in the area lie at Dougga in the hills west of Tunis. The hills around the ruined city are formed of marble, which has been quarried for centuries. The handy source of ideal building stone helped to make Dougga one of the finest cities of Africa and among the best preserved.

At the heart of the old city is the Forum, where the citizens met to conduct civic business. The magnificent columned square

is surrounded by various temples to gods as diverse as Fortune, Concordia and Saturn. But it is the Capitol which dominates the scene. The massive columned portico has remained in almost perfect condition. The carvings and reliefs almost as crisp as when first erected.

Not far away is the Temple of Caelestis, a local goddess, which has been largely rebuilt

with its huge limestone columns and broad platform. Further away is the theatre, now completely restored and in use again, complete with a car park.

South of the fertile coastal strip are the soaring mountains of the Tellian and other ranges. These effectively cut off the coast from the interior, except through a few passes and valleys. The spectacular beauty of these mountains has been recognized by the fact that several have been designated as national parks.

But it is south of the mountains that the desert comes into its own. Spread across thousands of square miles are long empty stretches of barren rock and sand. Only the occasional track breaks the feeling of utter emptiness. And few oases dot the landscape with their greenness against the interminable

brown of the desert.

The greatest area of sand desert in all the Sahara is the Great Western Erg, around the oasis of El Golea. This vast sea of sand covers well over 30,000 square miles and bakes in temperatures of over 100 degrees Fahrenheit. The wind of the desert blows steadily across the Erg, sometimes whipping up to high speeds which create blinding sandstorms.

The sand of the Erg has been piled up by the wind to form giant dunes known as barchans. Shaped into a crescent by the steady winds the barchans may be as much as 100 feet high and a mile in width. Perhaps the most disturbing aspect of the great dunes is that they move at a steady rate of around 60 feet a year. The wind drives the dune forwards, pushing each grain at a time, perhaps 20 yards each year. The sand Erg is gradually growing as it pushes on to engulf areas previously covered by rock. Several oases have already vanished beneath the shifting sands.

The coastal state of Tunisia (these pages) has a rich culture derived from Arab invaders of a thousand years ago. The Islamic faith of the newcomers is celebrated in the magnificent mosques (bottom) and (facing page) at Chenini. Left: A fisherman in traditional inshore craft. Top left: A street vendor. Above left: The Roman ruins of Dougga.

Beyond the Ergs, or sand seas, the Sahara is a strange and beautiful place. Tall mountain ranges with rugged peaks and towering cliffs are as common as the sand desert. But by far the greatest areas of the Sahara are covered by rocky plateaux and plains. Bare stone is covered by a layer of gravel or stones.

At Arak, on the edge of the Hoggar Mountains, stand some of the most magnificent gorges in the world. Sheer sandstone walls rise 1,600 feet from the dry floor of the canyons. The gorges were cut hundreds of thousands of years ago by a deep river running down from the mountains towards the plains. The gradual drying of North Africa which has been occurring for thousands of years, and still continues, caused the river to cease flowing many centuries ago. Today an eerie silence hangs over the gorges from which life has fled.

The Sahara is a dangerous land which is unforgiving of mistakes. Even today well-equipped parties can come to grief in the blistering heat of the searing desert. Yet the desert has its softer side, found in the densely populated oases which nestle beneath cliffs or between towering sand dunes.

On the northern fringes of the desert is the hollow of Nefta, where artesian waters bubble to the surface and form a magnificent waterfall down the slopes of the depression. Tucked away in the rich soil of the oasis are more than a quarter of a million date trees, each of which may provide 200 pounds of fruit.

The date is essential to the desert peoples and palm trees cluster thickly around any oasis in the Sahara. The fruit are a valuable source of food, but the usefulness of the tree does not stop there. The date stones are ground up to make a nutritious animal feed for the herds of sheep and goats kept by the nomads. The tough fibrous leaves can be dried and used to make baskets and matting. When a tree reaches the end of its 200 year lifespan it is felled for its timber.

Far to the south of Nefta the oasis of In Salah stands astride the old caravan route, and modern road which crosses the Sahara from the Mediterranean to the Gulf of Guinea. In Salah is the largest of the oases which lie in the depth of the desert. It is centered on a waterhole around which grow thousands of fruit trees. At the center of the town a small market provides a place where desert nomads can purchase fruits and other necessaries in exchange for their livestock and goods.

South of In Salah the road strikes out across hundreds of miles of emptiness known as the Desert of Thirst. It is nearly a thousand miles to the next reliable source of running water, the River Maradi. The roads here are little more than tracks, no attempt being made to supply a smooth driving surface. The tracks are better than the bare desert, but that is the best that can be said. Travelers only pass this way at their peril!

Yet to the people of the desert even this empty quarter is not devoid of life. At Agades

Northern and eastern Niger are dominated by the Tuareg tribesmen (above, center and facing page). Though occupying more than half the area of Niger, the nomadic Tuareg make up only a small part of the population. Nevertheless their warlike temperament has made them a considerable political factor, both during the French colonial period and since independence. The southwestern part of the nation is more densely populated by the agricultural Hausa people (left and top).

Above left: Children in the desert of northern Mauritania. Most of the country is desert and the desert peoples dominate society. Few places in Africa have such an evocative name as Timbuktoo. From the 12th to the 18th centuries this was a great center of learning and trade, being the greatest city for hundreds of miles. Today it has declined to become a town of mud brick houses and scattered patches of desert (left, above and top). Facing page: (top) Marrakesh and (bottom) Casablanca, both in Morocco. Overleaf: The Atlas Mountains.

in Niger is a sizable town based around a seasonal stream and wells. At Arlit a uranium mining town has sprung up around rich deposits. Mali's Gao is a fairly modern small town dropped into the desert complete with hotels and restaurants.

But these are only tiny islands of modernity intruding on the ancient world of the Sahara. The Tuareg, the proud people of the western desert, still roam the vast wastes, driving their herds of sheep and goats continually in search of fresh pasture land. They

move from oasis to oasis along ages-old routes and tracks across the empty desert.

In large part the Tuaregs retain their traditional culture. The families live in the large felt tents as did their ancestors. These tents are erected each time the family stops

and then taken down again as the family moves on. The clothing of the Tuareg remains equally traditional with the flowing robes and double face mask serving to keep out the desert sand carried by the wind which can sometimes howl across the landscape at frightening speed. It is a lifestyle superbly adapted to survival in the harshest of environments.

In religion the Tuareg are as fiercely Muslim as any other group of people. They have a proud adherence to their religion, a slightly individualistic version of the faith. Unlike the people of other Moslem countries the Tuareg accord women a high place in society. Indeed they were ruled by a line of Queens for many years. The most famous of these was Tin Hinan who may have lived around the year 300, or indeed at any time the Tuareg care to place her.

The trappings of the horses and camels ridden by the tribesmen are as colorful as the clothes of the riders. Brightly patterned tassels hang down from harnesses and saddles. The Tuareg remain magnificent horsemen, able to control their mounts with incredible precision. The horses are a reminder of the days when the Tuareg were a rule unto themselves, finding a living in many ways. Some less friendly than the pastoral

Morocco is predominantly Berber in culture. Small villages such as Oumsnat (this page), near Tafraout, are still governed according to traditional Berber laws and customs. At Marrakesh (facing page) the Berber culture mixes with that of the *Arabs. Overleaf: A village in the High Atlas Range.*

herding in which they now indulge.

The Tuareg were infamous as the most ferocious bandits in the Sahara. Large groups of Tuareg tribesmen would swoop down on caravans making the long, dangerous crossing of the desert. The hapless merchants would need to fight for their lives. Most often the attack would result in the death of the merchants and the theft of their goods.

But the Tuareg were not only bandits, they were also traders themselves and their favorite commodity was slaves. They would launch raids far to the south, carrying off negroes into slavery. To the Tuareg the negroes were infidels and savages who could be treated just as the Tuareg wished. The slaves were chained together and driven north across the Sahara to be sold in the slave markets of Algiers, Tripoli, Tunis and other towns. Thousands of unfortunates made the

The traditional transport of Morocco has for centuries been the donkey (below and center) and large donkey markets are regularly held in many towns. Along the coast fishing and fishprocessing employ many people. The fishing village of Essaouira (right and facing page top) has a sizeable fleet, but also has a flourishing tourist business due to its fine beach. Remaining pictures: Marrakesh.

journey each year.

The disruption caused to others by the traditional Tuareg lifestyle of raiding, herding and slave dealing survived up to this century, the wild desert tribesmen being a constant threat to the settled communities to both north and south. Their activities were only curbed by the appearance of more centralized states and effective means of self defence. But the Tuareg influence has remained strong. For instance, slavery remained legal in Mauritania until 1980 and is still, unofficially, widespread.

Even in other countries the tribesmen are treated with respect and their wishes taken into account when any desert policy is being decided. The desert would be truly empty without the heavily swathed, secretive Tuareg.

Hanging over the northern edge of the vast, arid wastes are the very different Atlas Mountains. The mountain slopes are blanketed by thick stands of cedar and pine interspersed with lush pasture land. The mountains reach up to 10,000 feet in height, forming a dramatic contrast to the desert below.

In places the scenery becomes startlingly beautiful. At the Forty Springs of the Oum er Rbia on the northern flank of the mountains a steep wooded valley forms the head waters of the Oum er Rbia river. The complicated

geology of the regions collects the rainfall from the high mountains and channels it underground to emerge in this charming valley. The slopes above the river are alive with gurgling springs and splashing waterfalls as the streams tumble down to join the main river.

Further south the violent but intermittent rivers of the desert-facing slopes have carved dramatic gorges from the mountains. At Dades the tumbling stream has carved a canyon 1,600 feet deep and so narrow that the sun rarely penetrates to the river. The rock walls of the gorge are rich in minerals. As the sun shifts across the rocks it produces a dramatic change in tone. The red hue of the cliffs changes through pale pink to glaring yellow in the mid-day sun before shading to the richest reds deepening to mauves as the sun vanishes across the western horizon.

It is in these scenically magnificent mountains that the Berbers continue with their ancient way of life. The Berbers are an ancient people who lived along the North African coast before the Romans conquered the area. Though pushed back from most of their homelands by waves of invading Romans, Phoenicians and Arabs, the Berbers retain their lifestyle in the mountains.

Here they tend their herds and live their isolated, remote lives. In Berber society nothing is prized so highly as freedom. Each

man is free and every village governs itself through a council of the eldest men. The central government of Morocco wisely leaves the Berbers much to themselves. Ill advised efforts by the previous French administration to impose its will on the Riff and Atlas led to decades of bitter warfare.

Nestling at the northern foot of the Atlas Mountains the city of Marrakesh forms a meeting place for the cultures of Northwest Africa. The city was founded by the nomadic Arab conqueror Abu Bakr in around 1060 as a market center for his expanding empire. It

These pages: Morocco. Facing page: Fields of grain give way to barren wadis, or dry river beds, at Ait Benhaddon. Right: The mountain village of Tinezouline. Top: The Atlas Mountains. Above and above right: Rabat, the modern capital of Morocco, which has a history dating back 2,000 years.

thrived immediately and became a bustling center for not only the Arabs but also the Berbers. Imported African slaves lent another cultural tinge to the city.

Though the city has since lost much of its importance it remains a fascinating place, rich in history and beauty. The most famous building in Marrakesh is the Koutoubia mosque. Begun in the 12th century, the mosque has been altered many times since. The great minaret was completed about 1190 when its dome brought its height up to 203 feet. It is visible from most areas of the town and is the area's most distinctive landmark.

On the coast the town of Casablanca is further removed from Berber influence and is more noticeably Arabic in culture. Like other coastal towns it has a distinctly European quarter dating from the French occupation. Here wide boulevards are lined by elegant houses. But there is also an old Arabic quarter and a modern shanty town which encircles the European-style heart and the busy port.

Rabat, like Casablanca, is a town with two sides. South of the Bou Regreg River is the French city built less than a century ago to be the government center for the colony of Morocco. It is a town of wide streets and modern buildings. North of the river is the old town with its narrow, twisting streets and traditional markets.

In many ways Rabat is typical of much of

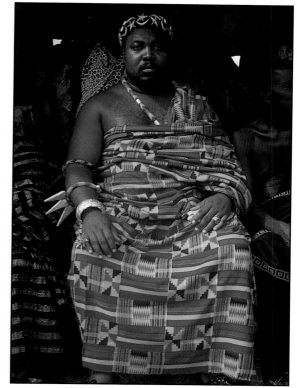

North Africa with its starkly contrasting modern face grafted on to the centuries-old culture embodied in the Islamic Arabs. Nowhere else is such a vibrant tradition existing alongside the modern world of technology and industry.

South of the great Sahara the lands grow increasingly moist and fertile. The barren desert shades away into scrub land which gives way to the open sahel. Here wide plains are covered by straggly grass and dotted by stunted thorn trees. The plains are used by local tribesmen as grazing lands for their herds of cattle which endlessly roam the dry landscape in search of fresh fodder.

The sahel stretches in a great belt across

West Africa from the coast north of the Senegal River to the lands around Lake Chad. It is a low, flat landscape swept by strong winds and rarely touched by rain. In recent years the lands have been growing gradually drier as the desert continues its millennia-old expansion from the north.

In Senegal the sahel is populated by nomadic Bassari tribesmen who drive their herds through the dry landscape. Like the more settled peoples further south the Bassari are followers of Islam, converted when the powerful Moroccan Empire pushed south across the Sahara five centuries ago.

It is in Senegal that the first major city south of the Sahara is to be found, Dakar.

These pages: Senegal. Facing page: At St. Louis, the northernmost city in Senegal, the sub-Saharan culture makes its presence felt with force, the colorfully dressed women being a strong contrast to the veiled women of Arab countries. The city serves as a base for visits to national parks famous for their birdlife. Right: The Presidential Palace in Dakar. The modern economy of Senegal relies on both traditional means, such as fishing (above) and on modern industries including phosphate mining (above right). Top right: A tribal chieftain in traditional dress.

With a population of over half a million Dakar is not only the national capital, but also a major industrial city for West Africa. It is heavily dependant on iron ore mined inland and on modern factories built largely with French money. The new shipyards are particularly important to the economy of this thriving city.

The modern city is built on a high promontory over the port where soft sea breezes sweep through the streets and past the European style buildings. On the lower land to the west, Dakar takes on a more African face. There are several markets where villagers come to town to sell their produce. The brightly dressed women with their basketwork and pottery make a colorful contrast to the fishermen just returned from the morning's trip. It is in this area of Dakar that the traveler first comes across sub-Saharan Africa.

Further from the desert the open sahel of Senegal gives way to the dense, humid forests of Sierra Leone and neighboring countries. In the dense jungles live a magnificent collection of wildlife, of a variety and splendor to be found nowhere else on earth.

The belt of dense coastal rainforest runs from the west coast of Guinea, through Sierra Leone, Ivory Coast, Togo, Benin and Nigeria to open out into the vast, trackless forests of Cameroon and the Congo River Basin.

The rainforest is quite unlike any other

habitat on earth, not only for its incredible variety of wildlife but also for the forest itself, a habitat locked into a self-perpetuating cycle. The dominant forms of plant life are the great trees which reach as much as 100 feet in height. These giants have tall, straight trunks which climb sheer before spreading out in a dense crown of branches which form an

Below: The idyllic beaches of Sierra Leone, a nation which began as a colony for freed slaves in 1787. Left: A colorfully dressed woman from the Gambia, a tiny nation consisting of little more than the banks of the Gambia River. Above and facing page: Traditional dances being *performed at Bijagos in the rainforest of Guinea-Bissau.*

evergreen roof to the forest floor. The light which filters through the trees casts an eerie green glow over plants and animals alike.

Below the canopy of great trees is a spreading understorey of saplings, bushes and shorter trees which find enough light in the perpetual twilight of the forest to survive. Finding a home in the trees and among the

undergrowth is a bewildering variety of animals.

In the upper canopy thrives a rich community of birds, insects and lizards. The birds are particularly colorful. The blue fairy bird cuts through the air in a flash of sky blue. The Gold Coast touraco shimmers in shades of blue, red and green as it flits through the branches. The Angola pitta has perhaps more shades than any other, its head being striped black and white, its body shading from emerald green through sky blue to scarlet and its tail a shining mass of blue and green.

But there are duller colored birds as well. The grey parrot lives up to its name with a uniform drabness broken only by its red tail. The much larger yellow-casqued hornbill has a remarkably drab black and grey plumage. It does, however have a quite remarkable nesting technique.

When the female is ready to lay she and her mate will search out one of the numerous holes in the tree trunks. She fills it with grass and foliage to form a soft nest. The male then blocks up the entrance with mud which quickly dries to rock hardness. Only a small opening is left through which the male feeds

Agidjan (above), capital of the Ivory Coast, is one of the most beautifully sited cities in Africa. It lies amid a collection of tropical lagoons separated from the Atlantic by sand spits and further palm-fringed lagoons. During the last century fever and disease were rampant here. Most settlers survived for only a few years before they died or were invalided home.

Recent health campaigns have reduced the death rate and the city now enjoys its reputation as a dynamic and scenic capital. Remaining pictures and overleaf: The peoples of inland Ivory Coast keep their culture alive through tribal dances, flamboyant costumes and markets featuring local goods and crafts.

the hen and the growing young. When the young birds are half grown, as much as six months later, the female breaks her self-imposed prison and flies free.

Among the many amphibians which thrive in the moist forests is the goliath frog, large enough to kill and eat mice and other rodents. The most remarkable lizard must be the famous chameleon, of which many species inhabit the forest. This slow-moving creature holds firmly to the twigs of the trees as it moves in search of its prey. The slow movements of the chameleon are deceptive for it can strike with lightning rapidity. Its enormously long tongue, almost as long as its body, can flash out to swat an insect in a fraction of a second.

The most famous feature of the chameleon is its ability to change color to suit its

background. Embedded beneath the skin are many pockets of coloring matter called melanophores. These vary in color from black to red and yellow. Signals sent by the eye, regarding the surrounding light conditions, cause these cells to expand or contract. If the eye detects the coming of night, for instance, the yellow cells will shrink while the black expand. Thus the skin becomes much darker.

The forest harbors a variety of mammals, perhaps the most unusual of which is the green striped squirrel, almost invisible in its forest home.

The forest floor is home to numerous browsers which feed on the bushes and saplings. Various ungulates find a home here, including the extremely rare bongo, seen by only a handful of outsiders, and the chevrotain, a tiny deer barely one foot tall.

It is ironic that one of the largest forest animals was only recently recognised by science. Before 1900 the travelers who reported coming across a strange antelope-like animal with striped legs were ridiculed and treated with scorn. Only when a naturalist named Harry Johnson came out of the West African forests with a skin did science take the claims seriously. They named the new animal the okapi and decided that it was related to the giraffe. It is possible that other animals still lurk in the forests, unrecognised by science. Local tribesmen repeatedly tell of a pygmy rhinoceros living in the inland hills, though nobody has yet succeeded in capturing one.

In West Africa, as elsewhere, the vast tracts of rainforest have begun to feel the pressure of an increasing population. In many areas this is restricted to forest management and the careful felling of areas in rotation. Elsewhere, however, the forest has been cleared for farmland.

Local tribesmen have been farming in the forest for generations. Some live in settled villages, where tribes have lived for centuries. Elsewhere slash and burn techniques are used. A section of forest is chosen, cleared and burnt. The ash adds to the natural fertility of the soil and ensures that the new clearing is able to produce crops for a number of years. When the soil loses its fertility the farmers move on to a fresh area and the forest returns to the clearing.

In the 1880s this picture of traditional agriculture was changed when a French planter named Verdier came to the newly acquired colony of Ivory Coast. He cleared the natural cover to plant a large fruit plantation which he farmed with all the benefits of 19th century technology. Today vast areas of West Africa have been cleared for the benefit of fruit plantations. In some areas it seems that no plant other than pineapples or bananas can survive. In other areas coffee and cocoa dominate the landscape.

It is these agricultural areas which largely

The tiny nations of Benin and Togo were the creations of European colonists. French settlers pushed inland from Porto Novo to create Benin (above) while Germans advanced from Lome to form Togo (left and below left). Both nations consist of a long thin strip of territory stretching inland from narrow coastlines. Ghana (below) and Nigeria (facing page) originated as British possessions. The people share a common culture, as can be seen from these pictures.

support the industrial towns and the ports such as Lagos, Takoradi and Porto Novo. The cities contain canning works, processing plants and docks through which the products are exported. In some nations of West Africa more advanced industries are beginning to make headway, but their progress is limited to a few coastal cities.

Despite the large upheavals brought about

by the expansion of cash-crop farming and the introduction of industry, the traditional tribal lifestyle of West Africa remains strong and fairly intact. In part this is due to the enormous influence of the various secret societies. These organisations trace their roots back to the days before European contact.

These societies have safeguarded the pagan religions of the region against both Moslem and Christian missionaries who have visited the area in past centuries. They have kept the tribes together, even when the people have become scattered.

Perhaps the major factor in the success of the secret societies is their claim to protect their members from the curses of the witch doctors. Though outsiders may scoff at such

powers they are taken very seriously in West Africa. In villages existing on the subsistence level and surrounded by dense, dangerous jungle the belief in spirits remains strong. Witch doctors, who claim to control these spirits, are greatly respected and feared. As recently as 1988 a witchdoctor was murdered by villagers on whom he had placed a curse.

Through such powerful beliefs the traditional crafts and skills of the region have been preserved. Today government sponsored schemes are producing various artifacts for sale to tourists and the age-old art of West Africa looks set to remain.

Among the most sought after objects are the wooden masks of the Ivory Coast. Most of these masks depict stylised animals and are used in various ceremonies and festivals. In

The lush rainforest which backs the West African coast is rich in wildlife, particularly insects. Above left: The hairstreak butterfly. Left: the giant silkmoth. Below left: The silkmoth. Below: The oleander hawkmoth. Facing page top: the citrus swallowtail butterfly. The drier grasslands to the north of the forests have an equally colorful, if less diverse, insect fauna, as is shown by the precis butterfly (facing page bottom).

huge expanse of land was the darkest area of the dark continent. Even today, when the area has been mapped by satellite, the empty land hides many secrets and mysteries from the prying eyes of civilisation.

Yet this great land is not a cohesive whole. It falls into two dramatically different regions, separated by the romantic and mysterious Ruwnzori Mountains.

To the west of the mountains lies the basin Ghana the goldsmiths produce beautifully decorated pieces while the ancestral stool occupies a place of especial esteem in the household.

West Africa is a land of forest and sahel where the past co-exists with the present in a remarkable mixture of cultures and traditions. It is a colorful land with its own excitement and charm found nowhere else in the continent.

Stretching across Africa is a vast belt of land, nearly a thousand miles deep and reaching from the mouth of the Congo to the mouth of the Rufiji Rivers, which is only sparsely inhabited by man. It is a strange land where the activities of humans have done little more than scratch the surface of the primeval world.

Indeed it was not until the 1860s that anyone passed this way who was able to write down his experiences. Until that date the

most travelers prefer to ignore such misleading information. Roads can be swept away in a single storm never to rebuilt. Most transport is by river as this is the only even remotely reliable way of getting around. Given such conditions its is scarcely surprising that the forest hides many secrets.

Among the wildlife which has flourished in this remote area are the African great apes. The smaller of these is the chimpanzee, which is equally at home in the trees or on the ground. During the day groups of chimpanzee scamper around the forest floor searching for fruit, leaves and other food. At night they will climb trees to build themselves nests where they will be safe from attack.

The chimpanzee may reach a height of five feet, which makes it considerably smaller than the gorilla, which inhabits the dense cover of the forest floor. A large male may be over six feet tall and weigh in excess of 600 pounds.

When rumors of the existence of the gorilla first filtered out of the forests it was reported to be a ferocious and extremely dangerous animal given to unprovoked attacks on man. Since then in-depth studies have revealed the giant ape to be a sociable, friendly animal with a complicated family life. Some naturalists have managed to become almost adopted members of a troop and have been filmed taking part in family ritual. It remains true, however, that an angry gorilla is quite capable of attacking and killing a human.

The basic social group of the gorilla is that of an extended family under the control of a large, dominant male. As many as forty gorillas might be gathered together in one troop. They eat a large quantity of food and remain constantly on the move in search of fresh resources.

Large areas of central Africa are covered by dense rainforest in which lives a wide variety of wildlife. Among the most interesting of these is the chimpanzee (below left and facing page). This ape is genetically very close to humans. Studies of genetic material suggest that the two may have shared a common ancestor as recently as 6 million years ago. Below right: A flimsy rope bridge crosses a river in the rainforest of Gabon. Above: Lake Victoria.

of the mighty Congo River. This 2,900 mile river rises in the 6,000 feet high Mitumbi Mountains before tumbling down an escarpment into the great basin which covers a huge area of central Africa. In all the river drains 1,500,000 square miles of mountain and forest, making this the largest drainage basin on the continent.

The majority of the basin is covered by dense rain forest. Routes through the dense forest are sometimes marked on maps, but

The largest of the great apes is the gorilla (these pages) which can reach over 6 feet in height and tip the scales at over 43 stone. The gorilla once ranged over vast areas of central Africa, but is now limited to a few patches of untouched rainforest and bamboo groves contained within national parks. There are two recognized subspecies of gorilla. The mountain gorilla (facing page and right) lives among the cool damp forests of mountains in Rwanda and Burundi. The more numerous, but still endangered lowland gorilla (remaining pictures) lives in the rainforest of the Congo Basin.

Left to themselves gorillas are content to travel slowly through the great forests, finding their food and molesting nobody. Only when they feel threatened do they show the more aggressive side of their nature.

Unfortunately the great apes are often threatened. Poachers and farmers can make money from killing gorillas and selling the bodies. Despite the efforts of game wardens and dedicated scientists the poachers are still at work and the gorilla remains an endangered animal.

The gorilla of the eastern forests was not recognised by science until the early years of this century and it remains possible that unknown animals still lurk in this vast forest. There is certainly plenty of space in which animals can hide.

Ever since European explorers began moving through the dense forests they have been told about a huge swamp reptile as large, or larger, than an elephant. Known by various names such as chipekwe, lau and mouroungou, the creature is said to have a large body and a long neck and tail. In 1919 an Englishman Captain Stevens set out to hunt the animal, convinced that it was a dinosaur. Unfortunately, he failed to find it. In the 1980s a team of American scientists set out to track down the beast. Though they found plenty of evidence that the locals believed such a creature existed, they failed to find the animal itself.

Equally mysterious in their way are the Ruwenzori Mountains which stand high above eastern flanks of the Congo Basin. Known locally as the Rainmakers, these mountains affect the weather of the lands around them. The range runs in a line for nearly 80 miles and reaches a height of

16,000 feet. This vast bulk forces the moist airstreams of central Africa upward, cooling them and creating clouds. The clouds drift away to deluge the area with rain.

In the mountains themselves the perpetual mist and damp atmosphere combines with the tropical heat to produce plants like no others on earth. There are lobelias which stand a staggering 20 feet tall and heathers twice as tall as that. Ferns, mosses and lichen cover every scrap of ground, making walking an eerily silent business in the Ruwenzori.

Below the eastern slopes of the mountains spread the wide open spaces of the East

add to its height.

The summit of Kilimanjaro is not the smooth plateau it appears to be from a distance. The top of the mountain is hollowed out to form a crater over a mile across where earlier eruptions carved away the heart of the mountain. Nor are the slopes as smooth as they seem, but broken and rugged.

In common with other mountains of East Africa, the slopes of Kilimanjaro are divided into distinct climatic zones, each of which supports its own type of vegetation and wildlife. At the summit of the mountain is the solid cap of ice and snow which is virtually devoid of life. Below the snowline, at around 16,000 feet, the bare rocky slopes of the mountain are dotted by small, ground-clinging plants producing bright yellow flowers. Only the smallest mammals, such as the

African savannah. The plains are cut and dissected by broad lakes and towering mountains. The greatest of the mountains is the famous Kilimanjaro.

The permanently snow-covered peak of the mountain reaches over 19,000 feet to the sky to make it the highest point in Africa. The mountain is a gigantic volcano which covers a base area of some 200 square miles. It has taken two million years of successive eruptions to produce this magnificent mountain. Future outbursts of cinder and lava can only

The imposing bulk of Mount Kilimanjaro (previous pages and facing page bottom) dominates the surrounding lowlands of northern Tanzania. The cool, wet flanks of the mountain are well-wooded and are densely planted with sugar and banana plantations (above). The lower slopes of the mountain and surrounding plains are hot and dry. Here live the Masai tribesmen (facing page top, top and above right) driving cattle on a constant quest for fresh grazing grounds.

hyrax and rats, survive here. They are preyed upon by high-flying eagles and hawks.

Below some 14,000 feet the bare rock gives way to open grassland dotted by scrubby trees and heathers. The russet-colored duiker, a small species of gazelle, crops the grass between the bushes where it keeps a wary eye open for the leopard, that most ubiquitous of African predators.

The leopard will also hunt in the mountain forest belt which extends as high as 10,000 feet. Amid the trees and bamboo thickets the leopard finds prey other than the diminutive duiker. There are larger antelope, together with ibex and baboons. The more adventurous leopard might even take young buffalo and rhinoceros in the depths of the forest.

In fact the leopard is a remarkably versatile animal which is as much at home in the chilly forests of Siberia as in the mountains of Africa. In most parts of its range this spotted cat is greatly feared as a maneater. Over a period of years one Indian leopard accounted for over 300 humans before it was shot.

At a variable height, somewhere around 5,000 feet, the mountain forest gives way to

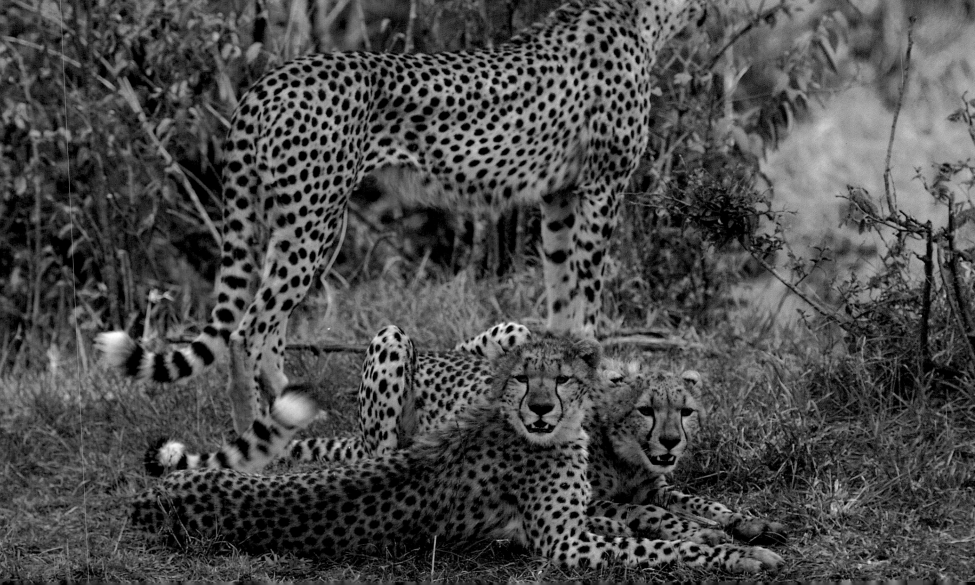

The vast dry plains of East Africa are famous for their big game animals. The leopard (previous pages) is a frequently seen predator. The cheetah (these pages) is rarer but more spectacular. This cat is acknowledged to be the fastest mammal on earth, but its exact top speed is unknown. Some authorities state that 65 miles per hour is the maximum, while others claim that the cat can top 80 miles per hour in short bursts. Overleaf: Giraffes.

the savannah, the landscape typical of East Africa. It is here that the animals most often thought of as being African live and thrive.

Spread across many hundreds of square miles of territory the great game animals form a unique society of animals perfectly adapted to the climate and vegetation of the region. Yet that is not to say that the wildlife is uniform throughout the region. Nothing could be further from the truth.

In an area the size of East Africa there is bound to be a variety of habitats and environments, each of which supports a different type of wildlife community. There are swamps, lakes and near deserts to be found on the plains, but by far the most typical environment is the savannah.

Savannah is the local name applied to the mixture of open forest and grassland which supports the richest community of wildlife. The grass is generally short, measuring

perhaps a foot in height, though it may grow tall enough to hide an elephant. There are dozens of types of grass on the savannah which mix in varying proportions in different places. In some areas red grass is so dominant that the ground can appear to be a shifting,

russet sea as the stems sway in the wind.

Here and there short trees dot the grasslands. For the most part these are rather scrubby and often covered with thorns. They provide little in the way of shade but provide convenient perches for leopards and lions.

In places the thorn bushes and trees grow densely together to form impenetrable thickets or dense forests. One such forest, some miles west of Gedi enjoyed an unenviable reputation earlier this century. The locals called the place 'Trees of Illusion,' and

maintained that anyone who entered became helplessly lost. The reason, it was said, was that the trees moved and changed position thus confusing the traveler.

The Europeans who hunted in the region during the years before World War I did not really believe the tales. One government official went so far as to offer to disprove the tales to the local tribesmen by entering the forest and then emerging a short time later. He became hopelessly lost. 'There was a queerly shimmering effect about the trees,' he recorded later, 'not unlike that of a mirage. There was a threatening effect, and I left as soon as possible.' It seems that there is more to the savannah than meets the eye.

On this mixture of open grassland and scrubby forest lives a wide variety of wildlife. The most dramatic, of course, are the big game. It is these animals which make up the unique community of the savannah. Every-

The national parks of Kenya are devoted to the preservation of the fauna of the dry savannah, each park having its own character. Ngorogoro is formed within a vast, collapsed volcanic crater and is famous for its birdlife; (top) flamingos.

The Serengeti (remaining pictures) is better known for its big game. Left, below and facing page bottom: A group of hippopotamos resting in water before emerging at dusk to graze. Above: A pack of wild dogs seize a

wildebeest by the nose before killing it. Facing page top: A wildebeest, or gnu, flees having been startled by the photographer. Overleaf: Zebra warily approach a waterhole.

thing depends on the plants of the plains. The herbivores eat the plants and are, in turn, eaten by the carnivores. Without the plants nothing could survive.

Among the plant-eaters is a rich diversity of animals, each suited to a particular way of life. Though they share the same environment and space they are not in direct competition with each other. Each species fills a niche on the savannah and thus avoids a mutually destructive search for the same food.

The smaller herbivores include the steinbok, a tiny antelope barely 18 inches tall at the shoulder. The reddish-brown coat of this animal is well suited to its habit of pushing through long grass or low shrubs. The even smaller dikdik confines itself to browsing on low-lying branches and twigs.

Another browsing gazelle is the elegant gerenuk which has disproportionately long legs and neck. The gerenuk feeds on the leaves of thorn bushes which it nibbles from between the wicked spikes with the aid of its delicate lips and narrow jaws. Unique among gazelles is its habit of rearing on its hind legs,

and resting its front legs on a bush for support, when reaching for higher branches.

The much larger kudu, which stands over four feet at the shoulder, is also a browsing animal. It is possibly the most beautiful gazelle of all. The delicately shaded coat is marked by vertical white stripes which break up its outline in wooded country. The true glory of the kudu, however, is to be found on his head. The twin, corkscrew horns which sweep backwards over its neck may measure

as much as three feet in length.

These horns ensured that the kudu was a favourite trophy amongst the big game hunters of yesteryear. But the kudu was far from easy game. Its ability to hide in dense cover was legendary. Even when sighted, the kudu might dash off at high speed or take to rivers and marshes where human hunters could not follow.

Out on the open grasslands the variety of antelope increases dramatically. Some graze

the ground the eland will nibble the leaves from the branches as if they were grass. This animal is both large and easily herded. Some efforts have been made to domesticate it as a replacement to cattle, but no great success has been achieved.

Perhaps the most surprising of the antelopes is the impala, which ranges widely across the grasslands from the Sahara to the Cape. Standing well over three feet tall at the shoulder, the impala is larger than most

Elephants, seen here in Kenya's Amboseli National Park, have a highly developed social life. The young are protected by adult cows (above, above right and top right) which keep them at the center of the herd where they will be safe from attack. The senior cow, or herd matriarch, will

investigate any intruder (facing page) prior to a false, but frightening charge (top left). If the intruder does not retreat, the herd may move off, or the matriarch may attack in earnest.

on the shorter grasses, others on longer stems. Some are able to survive on the brittle grass of the dry season, while other species have to move close to waterholes where the grass remains lush and green.

The largest of the grassland antelopes is the eland, which stands no less than six feet at the shoulder. Like the kudu, the eland is equipped with spiral horns, though these are noticeably less spectacular. As well as grazing the longer grasses, eland will use their horns to snap twigs from scrubs. Once they are on

gazelles. Though it is a grazing animal, the impala rarely leaves the shelter of cover. When it does stray from the bush it remains incredibly alert and will dash for safety at the least provocation.

It is during its run for cover that the impala reveals its surprise. Breaking into a headlong run the impala will suddenly leap high into the air. The animal can clear bushes and reach extraordinary heights. It is thought that the sudden, bone-jarring leaps are efforts to disorientate predators. Any lion faced by a

The semi-nomadic peoples who share the savannah with the big game have a remarkably complex and rigid social organisation. The Masai (below, bottom left and bottom right) are famous for their beadwork and their flamboyant ceremonial costumes. The Masai wedding party (bottom right) includes the groom, center, and his brother, right, the bride, left, is weeping as she is not allowed contact with her own family until she has produced a child. Right and facing page: The Samburu of northern Kenya who enjoyed a warlike reputation until earlier this century.

leopards. Both African species of rhinoceros are rare, but the more common of the two is the black rhinoceros.

This beast ranges across the grasslands of East Africa, though it has now been driven from much of its former range. It is a large animal, standing over five feet tall and weighing in excess of two tons. This formidable bulk is equipped with two horns sprouting from its nose. The front, longer horn averages about three feet in length, though horns well over four feet have been recorded.

a lethal weapon. The rhinoceros is all the more dangerous as its sight is extremely poor. It relies on scent for detecting enemies. When it gains a whiff of lion or man the animal will charge blindly upwind, attacking anything in its path.

The much larger white rhinoceros is, strangely, less dangerous. It is far less prone to charge without reason and spends most of its time moving through open forest and scrub grazing on the tough grasses. It stands over six feet and may weigh four tons.

It is interesting that the white and the black species of rhinoceros are actually virtually the same colour, a dull grey. No convincing explanation for the common names of these animals has been put forward. It may have something to do with the habit rhinoceroses have of rolling in mud to protect their skins

prey which suddenly leaps upward might well leave to search for easier victims.

All antelopes depend to some extent or other on escape to survive the attacks of predators. They may run, jump or hide in dense cover. But there are plant-eaters on the savannah which do not need to rely on flight for safety. Indeed, they may be counted amongst the most dangerous animals of the plains.

The rhinoceros is a massive animal whose aggressive behavior and formidable bulk means that it has little to fear from lions and

It is this horn which is the animal's chief weapon. When alarmed the rhinoceros will charge at whatever seems to be threatening it. The long horn, backed up by the massive impetus of two tons moving at high speed, is

from parasites.

Larger even than the white rhinoceros is the bush elephant which may stand as much as twelve feet in height and weigh six tons. Like the black rhinoceros, the elephant charges to defend itself, relying on its tusks as weapons. Usually, however these charges are bluffs, the elephant stopping short and snorting. When cornered, however, elephants will storm forwards, trampling and tusking anything in their path. Rogue males do not require any provocation to attack and have

been responsible for many human deaths.

Elephants have a highly complex family life, approaching that of humans and apes in its caring attitudes. From the moment of birth to the end of its life an elephant is part of a cohesive social unit.

When the female elephant goes into labour she retreats from the herd, to be followed by several other females. The little group stays together until the birth is over and the young is able to stand and follow its mother.

Throughout its early years the young elephant is carefully kept in the middle of the herd by the adults. There it is safe from attack by predators. As the young grows it takes its place in the herd.

Each herd is led by a senior female which leads the elephants on their constant journeying in search of fodder. The elephants eat such a huge quantity of grass and leaves that they are capable of stripping a small area in days and must then move on. Sometimes they will undertake migration marches of hundreds of miles in search of feeding grounds.

If ever an elephant is injured or gets into difficulties the herd will gather round to offer protection. More than one old-time hunter has been startled, on shooting a tusker, to find himself threatened by a dozen more. Even when an elephant dies, the herd will stay in the vicinity. Often they will try to push the corpse to its feet in a pathetic effort to revive their companion.

It is the elephants which have led to some of the more amazing stories to come out of Africa. Most of these can be traced back to observations of old-time hunters who knew the elephant in the field but had little interest

Previous pages: Storm clouds gather over Kenya's Masai Mara National Park marking the end of the summer dry season. Above and top: Ponds and streams are full during the rainy season. The modern face of Kenya is epitomized in the spreading tea gardens (facing page)
and the modern apartment blocks (left).

in formalised science.

It has been said that the elephant will stand up to a lion but flee from a mouse. In truth this is based on the elephant's fear of surprise. If it can see an enemy coming it will usually stand its ground. But when startled by the appearance of an animal, however small, it may start backwards and trumpet loudly.

The almost complete absence of elephant carcasses to be found on the savannah has led to the belief in perhaps the most romantic of all elephant legends; that of the Elephants' Graveyard. Though details vary from place to place, the legend remains basically the same.

It is said that somewhere, far away, is a cliff face with a narrow crack shattering its face. Through the opening runs a secret path, known only to elephants, which leads to a pleasant green valley around a lake. Here, the story goes, all elephants want to die. When

Along the low-lying Kenyan coast (these pages) the traditional lifestyle continues. The area has been strongly influenced by contacts with Arabs who sailed down the coast from the 16th century onwards in search of slaves and ivory. Overleaf: A village and, beyond it, the vast depression of the Great Rift Valley which stretches from Israel to Mozambique.

they feel ill or become old they travel to the cliff and the secret valley. They pass their last days in the happy vale before lying down amid the bones of their ancestors.

The story took on added importance due to the enormous value of elephant ivory. Anyone who could find the fabled Elephants' Graveyard could make a fortune simply by hauling away the tusks lying around in the valley. Unfortunately nobody has ever found the place.

The latest theory to account for the absence of elephant carcasses is that the herd buries their dead, or hides the body in thick undergrowth. In truth, however, the mystery remains.

Taller still than the elephant is the giraffe, the spindly wonder of Africa. A large male may top eighteen feet in height and weigh over a ton. The giraffe relies on flight to save it from attack. Its sight, smell and hearing are well developed, giving it plenty of warning of an approaching predator.

Generally giraffe live in small, loose-knit herds about two dozen strong which wander freely over the wooded plains. They feed not

The distinctive markings of the zebra might appear to make it extremely visible, but in fact it is a highly effective form of camouflage. For it to work the bold black and white markings rely on two other features. The first is that the creatures live in herds, the second is that lions are almost certainly color-blind.

The stripes on a zebra's coat run at an angle to the natural contours of the animal's body. The very boldness of the markings serves to disrupt the outline. When an entire herd of

The tribes of the savannah have a wide variety of ceremonies. The young Samburu warriors (facing page) must pass through various initiation ceremonies designed to ensure that they can protect cattle from animal or human predators, before they are counted as men. Left: a Chuka drummer leads fellow tribesmen in a war dance. Above: A Masai witchdoctor prior to performing an initiation. Below: A Pokot girl in ceremonial dress. Overleaf: Leaden skies over the savannah.

only on the leaves and twigs of trees, but also on the creepers and climbers which are festooned around their upper branches.

When in the open, giraffe often herd together with zebras and gnus, the other great herd animals of East Africa. The animals seem happy to cooperate, offering each other protection from predators. As with all herd animals, safety lies in numbers.

The gnu, or wildebeest, is one of the most numerous animals of the savannah and moves in vast herds, hundreds strong. It is a rather ungainly animal with a loping stride and a curiously unbalanced appearance. Despite the ox-like head and horns the gnu is actually an antelope. It feeds on medium length grass, thus escaping competition with its almost constant companion the zebra, which feeds on long grass.

As one of the few species of horse left in the wild, the zebra occupies an important place in East Africa. Like other horses, the zebra live in large herds, held together by a dominant stallion.

zebras is on the move it gives the appearance of being a mass of shifting black lines. It is very difficult to pick out the individual animals. To a lion, it is almost impossible. Yet it is only when it can single out a weak or young individual that the lion has a chance of making a kill.

The lion is, of course, the largest and most dominant hunter of the plains. A large lion may stand three feet at the shoulder and measure nine feet in length. It is a tawny sand color with a mane, usually rather darker and often extremely thick. This coloration, together with its habits, makes the lion almost impossible to see during the daylight hours. It will often spend its time resting in the shade beneath trees. When the lion ventures out on to the plains it keeps close to the ground, merging in with the long grass. Often the grass is burned yellow by the sun, a shade with which the lion's coat blends admirably.

Hunting most often at dusk, dawn or at night, the lion relies on being able to approach its prey undetected. When it has come as close as it dare, the lion will launch an attack of truly astounding ferocity. Unless the prey can escape within the first seconds of such a rush, it is doomed. Surprise is often gained by hiding beside waterholes, or alongside tracks. When a hapless antelope passes, the lion strikes.

Unlike most other cats, lions usually cooperate in the hunt. Prides of up to a dozen individuals will hunt together. One lion may deliberately move upwind of prey and make a clumsy attempt to approach them. The zebra, or other victims, will naturally move away from the hunter. With their attention fixed on the first lion, the prey do not see the others lying in wait until it is too late and the trap has been sprung.

Within the pride there is a distinct hierarchy. The male lions are at the top of the order. It is they who feed first and they who lead. The lionesses, however, seem to be

more active in the hunt. They will also look after the interests of their cubs at the risk of annoying the males.

As a rule lions have learnt to avoid humans, but this is not always the case. Occasionally a lion will take to man-eating, when it becomes a terror to the surrounding villages. One of the best known outbreaks of man-eating occurred late last century when the British were pushing a railroad inland across the Kenyan plains.

The workmen slept in various camps, surrounded by thorn fences, along the rail tracks. Quite suddenly men began to be killed and dragged from their tents by a pair of lions. Patterson, the British official in charge, constructed larger fences around the camps, but the attacks continued. On one horrific occasion the lions struck and dragged their victim to a nearby group of bushes. For some time the workmen could hear the lions noisily devouring their late co-worker.

After weeks of this nightmare, during which time dozens of workmen and local villagers were killed, the project was abandoned. The workers left the area in fear. Only after Patterson succeeded in shooting both lions could work continue.

Even today lions sometimes take to man-eating. There seems to be no explanation as to why some individuals take to this aberrant behavior. It is as well to remain wary of all lions.

The other cats of the savannah are solitary beasts, coming together only to mate. The leopard, a powerful predator, hunts by stealth. It may rest in trees, waiting for prey to pass beneath or it may prowl through long grass. When on the hunt the leopard reveals itself to be amazingly active. It will leap great distances, swim or sprint in the pursuit of food. It is, for its size, the strongest of cats.

Very different is the last of the great cats to frequent the plains. This is the cheetah, the running cat. Though it uses stealth to approach its prey, the cheetah relies on its amazing turn of speed to succeed in the hunt. In the final dash to the kill a cheetah may top 70 miles per hour for a few bounds.

This great speed is made possible by the structure of the animal's body. Its backbone is extremely supple and is able to bend and arch so as to give it a stride beyond the reach of others. The slender body is powered by muscular legs which are capable of developing quite extraordinary effort. If the first rush is unsuccessful, however, the cheetah will give up the chase and allow its prey to escape. Its muscles lack the stamina to keep up a long pursuit. Indeed, cheetahs have been known to abandon a run when only inches from their intended victim.

Like the plant eaters, the great cats are not in direct competition with each other for they hunt different prey in different ways. The lion tackles the larger zebras, gnu and buffalo. The leopard will take smaller antelopes when it can achieve surprise while the cheetah runs down the fleetest animals on the plains.

But it is not only the cats which hunt the plant eaters. Packs of hunting dogs roam freely across the grasslands, striking whenever they get the chance. Like lions they hunt in groups, co-operating closely and like lions

Lions, (this page) in Masai Mara and (facing page) in Etosha National Park, are the supreme hunters of the plains. They will tackle fully grown antelope and zebra and even take young elephants, risking the anger of the adults. However, they spend most of their time lazing in the shade. Only when driven by hunger do they hunt. Overleaf: Sunrise in elephant country.

These pages: Animals of Kenya's national parks. Above: The saddlebill stork, which gained its name from the bright yellow flap of skin which rests over the root of the bill. Above right: Defussa waterbuck. Right: A black rhinoceros, whose fearsome horn may reach three feet in length. Below right: An olive baboon, troops of which wander the plains in search of food. Facing page: A half-concealed leopard keeps watch for prey. Overleaf: A lone thorn tree awaits a coming storm in Nairobi National Park.

they prey on the larger animals such as zebras and wildebeest. The dogs are, if anything, more socially organised than the lions. They will take meat back to their permanent dens to feed young, who have meantime been guarded by other members of the pack.

The favorite tactic of the hunting dogs is to run a prey into exhaustion. When the victim tires they will close in from behind, snapping at the legs in an effort to disable the prey. Often one dog will leap for the tender nose in an effort to bring the animal to a halt. Then the others close in to kill. Unlike the swift neck bite of the cats, the dogs prefer to kill by numerous body wounds. This involves less risk to themselves, but makes for an

untidy and lengthy killing.

All these large predators are but the first rank among the meat eaters of the savannah. It is they who kill the big animals and are the first to feast on the carcasses, but they are not the only parts in the picture of predation on the plains.

Large carnivores, such as lions and dogs, will eat the most succulent parts of their kill. The muscular hindquarters and chest region are quickly devoured, together with the abdomen. When these choice parts have been consumed, the killer moves away. Their dentition is not able to pick at smaller pieces of meat. When hunger begins to gnaw, the hunter will kill again.

Meanwhile the abandoned corpse does not remain neglected for long. Scavengers, such as hyenas and jackals, appear first. Sometimes they arrive while the lions are still feeding. Usually the scavengers are content to wait until the killer has moved on. But if they are sufficiently numerous the hyenas may drive the lions away. Hyenas may also hunt on their own account, acting in packs, and lions are not above scavenging. The traditional roles of these two killers may sometimes be reversed.

The hyenas are well adapted to their

pieces of meat left on the carcass. The ugly birds pick at the bones, stripping them of the smallest piece of flesh. Their scrawny, naked necks are ideally suited to the task. They allow the bird to poke its beak into the deepest recesses of the corpse without feathers becoming blooded and matted.

When even the vultures leave, the carcass becomes a temporary home to various species of insect. These creatures are able to clamber inside the tightest of corners to reach flesh and materials which the birds cannot reach. There is even an insect able to eat the horns

lifestyle. They have extremely powerful jaws and strong teeth with which they can tear free the stringy meat of the forelegs and back. Hyenas can also use their jaws to snap bones and crunch the skeleton to get at the marrow which they love.

Jackals are nimbler and quicker than the hyenas. They delight in nipping in to grab a mouthful of meat and then retreating to the safety of cover. Between them the jackals and hyenas will reduce the larger sections of muscle.

Next on the scene are the vultures. Circling endlessly in the clear air, the vultures are able to locate a kill at a distance of many miles. While the scavenging mammals take the best of the pickings, the vultures gather around in an ominous ring.

They move in to take advantage of the final

Top: A flock of white pelicans swoop low over a lake in Nakuru National Park. Above: A herd of Burchell's zebra comes to drink. Of the three species of zebra, Burchell's is by far the most common. Left: A pair of impala bucks lock horns in a rut while a third looks on. Facing page: An ever watchful cheetah studies the photographer for a hint of danger. Overleaf: A herd of impala look up from grazing.

of gazelles. Within a day only a scattered collection of bones remains of a living creature.

This unique and formidable collection of wildlife developed on the East African plains over a period of millions of years. The climate and environment of the region has barely changed in 12 million years, perhaps even longer. In this enormous time a number of animals, each superbly adapted to the circumstances has developed to form a highly complex and delicately balanced community.

One of the animals which developed here some four million years ago has now come to dominate the rest. Humans first appeared in East Africa, their fossils being uncovered by modern scientists in recent years. For many years man simply fitted into the pattern as an opportunistic feeder taking both plant and animal food whenever he could.

Later, man began to have a more direct influence on the wildlife and the environment. Various tribal groups appeared which developed a culture well adapted to the savannah.

In the drier districts the people remained hunters, but also imported cattle and goats which they herded across the grasslands. Inevitably this led to friction with the wildlife. Lions and leopards took cattle while antelope were direct competitors for grazing.

Beadwork is made much of in Africa while tusks and animal teeth are used for a variety of purposes. These costumes are amongst the most colorful and attractive in the world.

Throughout most of the region the tribes lived in loosely connected groupings. Warfare was endemic and in some areas large kingdoms were built up by energetic tribes. This traditional scene of pastoral and agri-

cultural activity was disrupted by the arrival of colonising Europeans.

The first strangers to arrive, about a thousand years ago, were the Arabs who settled various coastal sites. From here they launched expeditions into the interior, hunting for ivory and for slaves. Both were taken in large quantities from the tribal lands. Western European ships called along the coast from the 16th century onwards, in increasing numbers. But it was not until the later 19th century that any serious attempt to penetrate the hinterland was made.

By the 1880s British and German traders and missionaries were pushing inland and making contact with the tribes. Between 1888 and 1894 the European powers established protectorates over East Africa and set about increasing the productivity of the region.

The favored means of doing this was to import cash crops from elsewhere, grow them on a plantation system and then sell them abroad. By far the most successful of these crops' were coffee and tea, taking a share of the market away from the crops traditional homes. But the process was slow. As late as 1911 a comprehensive view of the world tea industry could devote several pages to Natal and Paraguay, without giving East Africa even an entire paragraph to itself.

Today the situation is very different.

Facing page top: White backed vultures move in to strip a wildebeeste carcass of its remaining flesh as an hyena prepares to leave. Facing page bottom: A vast flock of flamingos rest in shallow water. Top: A crowned crane. Left: A vervet monkey. Below: Nubian vultures gather for a gruesome feast. Above: A curtain of rain sweeps across Masai Mara National Park towards a safari.

Both groups suffered from the tribesmen, but survived in large numbers.

In moister areas farming was a practicable proposition and permanent villages sprang up. These villagers also hunted and herded, but to a lesser extent. Crops were grown to satisfy local demands and most of the population existed on a subsistence level.

The tribes built up a rich culture, characterized by distinctive artwork and dances. The greatest glory of the culture is often thought to be found in the dances and ceremonial costumes. Cloaks of animal skin and headdresses of feathers are common and dramatic.

Thousands of acres are under tea gardens, and nearly as much land devoted to coffee plantations. Kenyan tea is much in demand by blenders as it adds strength and astringency to the more delicately flavored teas of highland India without greatly affecting their flavor.

Though the new crops of tea and coffee dominate the agricultural scene, the older farming activities have not been neglected. The application of more up to date practices have breathed new life into the traditional crops. Cattle farming is now turning a handsome profit and dairy products feature

Above: When the dry season is at its height large herds gather around the few remaining pools of water. Here buffalo muddy the waters in Tsavo National Park. Left: An ostrich stalks Samburu National Park. Below: A pair of rare African fish eagles perched beside Kenya's Lake Baringo. Facing page top: A black rhinoceros moves across Amboseli National Park beneath Mount Kilimanjaro. Facing page bottom: Sleeping flamingos at dawn.

regularly on export figures.

Along the coast the traditional fishing business has boomed in recent years to meet demand from the new cities. Fishermen who previously caught only enough to feed themselves and their families now catch fish to sell for cash, with which they can buy themselves a better standard of living than their fathers enjoyed.

In the cities of Mombasa, Nairobi, Kampala and Kigoma the population has risen as industrialisation takes firm hold of the area. Much of this industry is, of course, based on the agriculture of the region. There are tea, coffee and tobacco processing plants together with grain mills and sugar mills. However some of the industry is based on the mining of various minerals. There has also been a rise in consumer industries, such as clothing,

leather works and motor spares.

Nairobi, the largest city of central Africa, did not come into being until 1900, when it was a railway station and a few houses. There is, of course, little of historical interest here, but the city has a thriving business district and many monuments to the dynamic face of today's East Africa. There are the Parliament Buildings of 1955, which are open to the public and adorned with traditional art, and the modern university which teaches a wide range of skills. The Railway Museum shows the importance of the expansion of the rail network to Kenya while the National Museum highlights the wildlife and traditional cultures of the country.

In all the modern bustle and technological advance of East Africa it is comforting to know that the glorious wildlife has not been

neglected. All nations of the area have established National Parks, among the best in the world, where wildlife is protected. If the recent anarchy in Uganda led to an outbreak of poaching, the situation seems to be back under control and the other nations have protected their wildlife. In some areas it is possible to see the game animals wandering the plains outside the National Parks.

One of the most popular parks for visitors, certainly the most scenic, is Amboseli which lies on the lower slopes of Mount Kilimanjaro. The land is generally flat and the trees well spaced out. This allows visitors good chances of seeing game such as the elephants, giraffes and lions which thrive in the area.

Less popular, but more like the untouched Africa, is Meru. There are no sealed roads within the park and the dirt tracks degenerate

Chameleons are among the commonest and most unusual animals in Kenya. They have the ability to change color and can move each eye independently. Top left: A high-casqued chameleon. Left: A dilepis chameleon. Top right: A bearded chameleon shedding its skin. Above: A graceful *chameleon devouring an insect. Facing page: A dragon fly emerges from its larval skin.*

after heavy rains. The grass here is very high and conceals all but the larger animals. Nevertheless it is a fine place for the more adventurous. By far the largest park is Tsavo which flanks the Galana River north of Mombasa. It contains perhaps the finest game herds of all, and is the site of the depredations of the man-eating lions fought by Patterson last century.

But the most spectacular parks of all are to be found to the south in Tanzania. Serengeti covers a vast area south of Lake Victoria and is famous for its large herds of zebra, gnu and antelope. The nearby Ngorogoro Crater consists of the hollow crater of an extinct volcano which covers some 110 square miles of the finest grazing country in the area.

It is interesting to note that the grand old style of hunting safari is still operating in some areas of East Africa. Exactly how many of which animals are allowed to be shot each

Though often neglected by visitors, the reptiles of the savannah are every bit as interesting as the big game. Left: A hatchling gecko emerges from a nest. Below left: A red spitting cobra. Below: A ridged frog. Bottom left: The deadly puff adder. Facing page top: An African rock python. Facing page bottom: A savannah monitor killing a spitting cobra.

year is carefully controlled by conservation authorities and stiff penalties meet anyone who oversteps their allowance. It is also an extremely expensive operation. By the time game fees have been paid together with wages for guides, bearers, beaters and cooks and park charges a prospective hunter may find that he has parted with $20,000. And there is no guarantee that he will actually get to shoot anything.

Hunting has now been banned in most reserves, though some culling takes place almost everywhere. The ban upset many who made a living from escorting hunting parties, but it now seems that far more money is to be made from tourists with cameras than from hunters. For this reason, if no other, the magnificent wildlife of East Africa seems to have a secure future.

Southern Africa is a land dominated by three great rivers, the Zambesi, the Limpopo and the Orange. Together these rivers drain most of the southern third of the continent. They draw their waters from a land startling in its contrasts. There are vast swamps, feet deep in mud and burning deserts which do not see rain from one year's end to the next. There are plains teeming with a wildlife unequalled anywhere in the world, and there

Previous pages: Sunset over the lower Zambezi River. These pages: The *Zambezi hurls itself over the Victoria Falls, creating a massive plume* *of spray and a near-permanent rainbow. Overleaf: Elephants* *trudge across the arid Chote in Botswana.*

are cultivated fields stretching to the horizon where no wild animal larger than a mouse can find a home.

Of the three great rivers the longest and most magnificent is the Zambezi. It rises on the high Angolan plateau some 1,300 miles from its entry into the Indian Ocean. Here, on the tall grass savannah, can be found some of the most magnificent wildlife on the continent. Elephants push through the soaring stems, which can hide them completely

the Zambezi abruptly changes direction and character. Turning east the river plunges into the Dundari Hills and then forms itself into one of the most stupendous natural wonders in the world.

North of Wankie, the Zambezi hurls itself over a precipice to form the Victoria Falls. The falls are 420 feet tall and stretch over a mile in width. At the peak of the rainy season nearly a quarter of a million gallons of water plunge down the cliff each second.

Facing page: The Okavango Swamp and (this page) some of its birdlife. Left: A crimsonbreasted shrike. Right: A great white egret and chick. Below left: A lilacbreasted roller. Below: A blackheaded creole.

from a distance of just a few feet, and leopards prowl the undergrowth.

From the high plateau the young river tumbles down the steep flanks to flow southward across vast plains, very similar to the savannah and scattered thorn of East Africa. The wildlife is similar, too, with antelopes and zebra moving in large herds, preyed upon by lion and cheetah.

At Katima, a stopover town on one of the main routes crossing Africa from east to west,

The thundering, spray-drenched spectacle is made more impressive by the fact that the river drops into a chasm barely 250 feet wide. The churning, foaming waters struggling for space at the bottom of the abyss is a sight few can forget. This narrow gorge channels the tremendous amounts of spray directly upward, forming them into a column over 1,000 feet high. The spray drifts away gently on the breeze, drenching the surrounding area in an almost perpetual rainfall.

The local name for the falls is Mosi-oatunya, which translates as 'the smoke which thunders.' The European name was given to the falls by the famous explorer-cummissionary Dr Livingstone who passed this way on a nightmare journey of hunger and disease in 1855. Though suffering great hardships, Livingstone was so moved by the sight that he wrote in his diary 'scenes so lovely must have been gazed upon by angels in their flight.'

Livingstone was the first man to travel the entire length of the Zambezi. At the site of the present town of Kasane, Livingstone came across a major tributary, the Okavango. He followed the stream southwest until he was stopped by a huge sea of reeds, mud and swamps. For some weeks Livingstone cast around to north and south, hoping to find a route around or through the swamp, but to no avail.

What Livingstone had found were the fringes of the mighty Okavango Swamp, 7,000 square miles of the most amazing territory in Africa.

The swamp is that most unusual of natural features a delta without a sea. Instead it flows into a desert. The Okavango River rises on the Angolan Plateau, not far from the headwaters of the Zambezi and follows a roughly southeasterly course for some 600

Facing page: A herd of elephants comes to drink at Botswana's Chobe River at sunset. Top: A pair of zebra pause in their grazing on the arid grasslands. Above: Impala at sunset. Right: A hippopotamos returns to the sheltering waters of the Okavango after a night's foraging on dry land.

miles before dividing at Parakes. One branch runs east to join the Zambezi, the other turns south towards the scorching Kalahari Desert.

The southerly branch travels barely fifty miles before flowing on to a huge open plain of almost uniform flatness. Here the waters spread out to form a thousand channels and streams which weave and cross their way southward. The waters bring down millions of tons of silt each year. As the streams gradually slow down the mud drops out to the bed, blocking the streams and slowing them even further. It is this which has formed the great swamps.

The heat is intense and the placid waters are sucked up by the sun. Less than one tenth of all the water which enters the swamp makes it through to the southern fringes. Beyond the swamp the land drops down toward Lake Ngami where the overflow collects. When exceptionally heavy winter floods affect the Okavango some waters spill over from Ngami to run southwards to the Makagadikgadi Saltpans where they are finally evaporated by the sun.

The swamps themselves are a haven for wildlife. It is a collection rarely seen elsewhere in Africa for here the savannah animals mix freely with the water wildlife. This strange mixture is due to the seasonal rainfall which affects the area. During the dry season the surrounding grasslands are scorched by the sun while the water level in the swamps drops dramatically. Dry ridges are exposed, where lush grass grows profusely.

In October the big game from surrounding lands moves in to the drying swamps to take advantage of the sweet water and abundant foods. The great herds are, for four short

These pages: The Nguni peoples of southern Africa lead a life still dominated by the past, though influenced by modern developments. Left: A kraal, or family home, made up of traditional round beehive huts and a mud hut built square so as to resemble town buildings. Bottom: A youth collecting firewood. Remaining pictures: Traditional costumes.

months gathered together in a concentration which few find unimpressive. Lions, leopards and hyena come together in the swamps to take advantage of the almost unlimited food supplies.

As summer turns to autumn, heavy rains on the Angolan plateau raise the level of the Okavango which pours its surplus into the swamps. In a matter of weeks the water levels rise dramatically, flooding the summer grasslands and turning the whole area into a vast morass. The water animals, confined during the dry months to isolated pools and streams, spread out to inhabit the entire swamp. Waterplants burst out in a tangled mass of growth which makes the swamp unique.

Wherever the water is shallow enough papyrus reeds clog the waterways. Growing over head-high on a man the reeds block both the view and any movement. Elsewhere floating waterferns form a solid mat on the water which, in places, is strong enough to support a man.

Virtually the only way of moving through the swamps is by makuru, the local style of canoe propelled by punting. Traditionally made of wood, the makuru rented out to

visitors are now increasingly made of fibreglass, virtually the only sign of modern civilisation in this primeval landscape.

In places, where the swamp growth is particularly dense the makuru men can only make progress by the hazardous method of poling along hippotracks. There is always the chance of coming unexpectedly across one of these large animals, and the risk that it will upset the canoe. Such an event might prove disastrous in such a remote area.

Nonetheless the stupendous variety of wildlife visible from the makuru makes the trip worthwhile. Basically the wildlife of the Okavango is similar to that to be found in rivers, lakes and swamps throughout southern Africa, but it occurs on a scale totally unique.

Though elephants may sometimes frequent the edges of the swamp the largest true swamp dweller is the hippopotamus, originally found throughout Africa from Cairo to the Cape, but now rare in many areas. Standing some five feet high, the hippopotamus may weigh over four tons.

On land it moves around on heavy, pillar-like legs which seem scarcely able to support its weight. But in the swamps this lumbering giant becomes a creature of grace and elegance. The surrounding water almost cancels

Previous pages: A flock of greater flamingos flying over Namibia's Sandwich Bay. Facing page: A female greater kudu and young. The female lacks the spectacular twisted horns of the male. Top: Impala. Left: A vervet monkey. Above: A group of chacma baboons indulging in communal grooming. Such grooming not only removes parasites but also forms part of a complex system of establishing and enforcing social positioning.

out its weight, and the creature glides easily along. It keeps to densely reeded areas, pushing its way through the foliage with its enormous bulk.

The hippopotamus feeds on the long reeds and swamp plants which choke the Okavango, but it may also emerge at night to feed on grasses which fringe the deeper water. To crop grass and shred tough rushes, the hippopotamus has a fearsome array of teeth. The most dramatic of these are the tusk-like canines over two feet long. Behind these are a battery of grinding teeth well adapted to pounding up the tough fibrous stems of the water cabbage and other plants.

Moving through the drier areas of the swamp is the sitatunga, or swamp antelope. This elegant little creature moves nervously through the shallows, grazing on reeds and other wetland plants. Its graceful horns can often be glimpsed moving above the level of the reeds, which the rest of the creature is hidden by the dense foliage.

The sitatunga, and indeed other swamp creatures, must remain constantly on the alert for the undisputed hunter of the wetlands, the crocodile. The African, or Nile, crocodile is a large animal. An old individual, anything up to a century in age, may be as much as 17 feet in length.

The crocodile spends most of its time in deceptively sluggish mood. It may cruise slowly through the water, paddling its way

forwards with its long, swirling tail. At other times the crocodile will rest on the sandy spits of the swamps and rivers as if asleep. Often it rests with its long, ferocious jaws gaping open. Tickbirds scurry around the sleeping giant, picking insects and parasites from the hide of the reptile. Some birds will dart inside the crocodile's mouth itself to pick scraps of food from between its teeth.

But when hungry, or when food is to be had, the crocodile becomes a very different, more active animal. Raising its body clear of the ground, the animal can run faster than a

man, while in the water it can power itself forwards at frightening speed when completely submerged.

Having located a prey, the crocodile strikes quietly. A deer come to drink, or a bird wading in the shallows, may not be aware of the presence of the reptile until it is within a few feet. In a fountain of spray and mud the crocodile surges forward, seizes its prey and then retreats to the water, pulling its catch down to the depths. Only the swirling waters remain to mark the death of another victim.

Beneath the water, the crocodile waits

These pages: The ubiquitous leopard which is found across the whole of Africa, and much of Asia. Leopards are good climbers and often rest in trees. If a potential victim passes beneath it, the leopard will drop directly on to its back. More than one game park in Africa has notices warning visitors not to walk beneath trees. Overleaf: Acacia trees at sunset.

merged log and wait for putrifaction to set in and loosen limbs.

Count Byron de Porok, a traveler who passed through Africa in the years before the First World War, saw the crocodiles before modern guns and traps brought about a huge reduction in their numbers. He was told that one large river village expected to lose about twenty people to the reptiles each year. The locals seemed undisturbed by the toll, accepting it as part of life. After all, armed with only spears, there was little they could do about the problem.

Today intensive hunting of crocodiles for their precious skins has resulted in a catastrophic decline in crocodile numbers. They have been exterminated in many areas and hang on only in reduced numbers elsewhere. The slaughter has been condemned by conservationists and scientists, but the passing of the crocodile is hardly likely to cause concern among the local tribesmen. They no longer need fear going to fetch water.

The larger mammals and reptiles are spectacular animals, but the true splendor of Okavango wildlife are its magnificent birds. Dozens of different species thrive in the swamps, filling the air with their calls and the whispering softness of their wings in flight.

Various species of saddlebilled stork are to be found in wetlands throughout Africa. Standing anything up to five feet in height and having wingspans of ten feet or more, the saddlebilled storks are among the most spectacular birds of the Okavango. The jabiru saddlebill is a particularly striking bird, with a boldly marked white and brown body and

Above: A herd of elephants enjoying a mud bath. Dried mud helps to protect the elephants' hides from ticks and other parasites. Buffalo also suffer from parasites. Left: A buffalo welcomes a redbilled oxpecker which feeds on skin parasites. Below: A chaca baboon yawns, revealing an impressive

set of teeth. Facing page: A pair of giraffes in Londolozi Game Reserve in South Africa. Overleaf: A rare family group of cheetahs, which are usually found as solitary animals.

until its prey stops struggling, then changes its grip. Sometimes a crocodile will swallow a small prey animal at once, but larger victims require more careful handling. Crocodiles cannot chew, they must bite off pieces small enough to swallow in one go. When this cannot be done, the crocodile may spin at speed, hoping to twist a piece of flesh free. Or it may lodge its victim beneath a sub-

black neck. The bill itself is bright red, with a black stripe and yellow skinflap.

The closely related marabou is a far less attractive bird, with its scaly, featherless head and neck and a plumage of black and white. The marabou soars over the swamps, keeping an eye open for carcasses and rotting flesh. Having spotted food, the carabou swoops down, gathering in large groups to perform the function taken by vultures on the plains. British soldiers stationed in Africa last century coined the name of Adjutant Stork for the carabou, a caustic comment on the strutting walk and fussing behavior of the bird and their staff officers.

The swamp birds display a remarkable diversity of bill shape and size, each adapted to finding food in the swamps. The roseate spoonbill, as its name might suggest, has a bill shaped like a spoon. The narrow root of the bill forms the 'handle' while the broad, rounded tip is the bowl of the spoon. The bird wades through shallow waters, swinging its bill from side to side, filtering out crustaceans which it then swallows. The closely related ibis has a beak which curves downward in a graceful sweep. It hunts the fish which swarm in the warm, shallow waters.

But perhaps the most amazing of the

The birdlife of southern Africa is justly famous, being both diverse and colorful. Above: An African fish eagle snatches a victim from the waters of Zambia's Lake Tanganyika. Left: A group of greater flamingos lifts off from Walvis Bay. Right: A chanting goshawk perched in a tree in the eastern Transvaal. Facing page: A greenbacked heron prepares to swallow a catch.

African swamp birds is the shoebill. Rarely seen south of Burundi, the shoebill is specially adapted to life in the papyrus swamps. Its body is unremarkable, being similar to that of a stork and colored a dull grey. But its bill is a truly noteworthy organ. The long, deep bill seems far too large for the bird, but is essential for rooting in the thick, glutinous mud of the swamps. Here the shoebill finds a wide variety of frogs, invertebrates and that most unusual of swamp creatures, the lungfish.

The African lungfish, of which there are four species, has a torpedo shaped body, with a powerful flattened tail. It haunts swamps and slow-moving water, where it hunts the bottom-dwelling fish which live in or on the

deep beds of mud. During most of the year, the fish behaves like other fish, taking in oxygen from the water by way of gills. But when the dry season comes around and many rivers and lakes empty of water, the lungfish reveals its peculiar adaptation.

When waters become shallow, the fish digs itself a deep, egg-shaped burrow. The hole is filled with a special mucus, the outer layers of which dry to rock-hardness. Only a small hole at the top of the burrow is left open. Through this tiny opening, the lungfish draws in air, which it breathes. To do this the lungfish has a pair of simple, sac-like organs which are lined with corrugations and mucus. These organs, commonly called lungs, seem to be developed from the gill

pouches which most fish lose while still embryos.

The lungfish can survive in its sealed burrow for many weeks, even months. As soon as the waters return, the hard mud and mucus casing dissolves. The fish breaks free and resumes its active hunting life.

The more open waters of lakes and rivers which are free from the clogging effects of papyrus, lilies, water ferns and water cabbages offer a very different habitat and support a quite different variety of birdlife.

The most picturesque of these are the flamingos which gather in tremendous flocks containing millions of birds. The spindly figures of the flamingos are most often seen pacing slowly through the shallows, their

Like most cats, leopards prefer to drag their victims to a secluded spot before beginning to eat. The leopard (left) having killed a small antelope in the darkness is dragging it into a tree before she, or her cubs, begin to feast. Below left: A lion grotesque after a prolonged mud bath. Bottom left: Another, cleaner lion, in the act of killing a warthog by the favored, and highly efficient, throat grip. Facing page top: A lioness with her cubs. Facing page bottom: Sunset over a thorn tree in the Londolozi Game Reserve of South Africa.

heads down in characteristic feeding pose, or standing with one leg tucked beneath the body for hours at a time.

A large flock of flamingos is one of the most unforgettable sights in Africa. At rest, the flock appears to be a shifting sea of pink and white. When startled, the birds raise their necks giving the impression that a wave has swept across the flat expanse of the flock. If danger threatens the birds begin to run, moving unerringly in one direction. As their speed increases the broad pink wings, with

black strips reach out and begin to beat the air. Then the birds are airborne, climbing high in a spiralling climb which carries them upwards and out of danger.

There are, in fact, two distinct species of flamingo on the African lakes. The common flamingo is the larger of the two and is sometimes known as the greater flamingo. It dips its beak into the water, stirring up the fine mud to filter it of tiny invertebrates. It may even take small fish if they can be found.

The lesser flamingo is slightly smaller and feeds on different food, thus avoiding competition with its larger cousin. The shorter, deeper beak of the lesser flamingo is used to filter the surface waters for green algae. The upper bill is fringed with a comb of thin membranes known as laminae. The water is sifted through this and food particles caught on the surfaces of the laminae. The bird then licks up the food and swallows it.

South of the spreading Okavango Swamp is the great Kalahari Desert, a land of sparse scrub and seasonal grassland. It is in this barren trackless expanse that the original human inhabitants of southern Africa still find a home they can call their own.

The Bushmen are a race apart from the others of Africa. They are short and have light-brown skins with pointed chins and wiry bodies. The most remarkable physical characteristic of the Bushmen is that their buttocks are large and heavy, acting as fat storage organs. They have no generic name for themselves, only recognising such tribes as the Balala or Bakwena.

Inhabiting lands totally unsuited to any form of agriculture or pastoralism, the Bushmen rely on harvesting the wildlife for food. They move more or less constantly in search of fresh feeding grounds. If they find a place which promises to support them for some time the Bushmen will erect a hut made of

branches braced into a cone and covered by long grass. Otherwise simple shelters of grass suffice.

Women and men have distinct and equally vital roles in the society. Women look after the children and stay close to the camp site. They gather insects, reptiles and seeds which can be taken back for food. The men, meanwhile, leave the camp to hunt larger game. Traditionally they used small bows and heavy spears but in recent years a few families have acquired battered old muskets and a precious store of gunpowder.

When a small antelope is sighted, the men creep forwards silently with all the skill which comes from continual practise. When they have come close enough, the men let fly with arrows or guns in an attempt to cripple the prey. An uninjured antelope can outstrip the hunters, but a wounded creature will soon tire. When the victim stumbles, the men pounce with their spears and swiftly complete the kill.

It is a precarious existence for the Bushmen, but one which they have followed for millennia and, left to themselves, will continue for many years to come.

Around the Kalahari spread huge areas of open plains and rolling hills which are covered by lush grazing land and open forest. On these more verdant lands thrived great herds of game, but centuries ago these were largely replaced by the cattle herded by the Nguni peoples.

The basic feature of the Nguni lifestyle is the kraal, or village. Each kraal is the center of a social grouping, be it a family, a tribe or a kingdom. The houses, generally known as 'beehives' are made from long, tough grass which grows on the plains. The grass is cut to the required length and then bound together in a number of ways.

Tough, solid bundles are used as supporting frames for the hut, though in areas with

The Bushmen, the original inhabitants of southern Africa, lead a semi-nomadic life as hunter-gatherers on lands unfit for grazing or agriculture. Facing page: The men of a band leave camp armed with spears and bows and arrows, and (top left) they return with a bustard, the heaviest flying bird of the region. Above: Women prepare vegetable food, such as tsamma and baobab fruit. Left: Evenings are spent beside the fire eating, talking and making tools.

plentiful trees wood might be used. The framework is circular in plan and domed so as to give the greatest natural strength to the design. The outline supports are then filled in with smaller bundles of grass and thatching. The whole is held together by ropes of twisted grass. The finished structure is remarkably comfortable. The thatching keeps off the heavy rains of the area while the open structure of the walls allows breezes through to cool the interior during the hot summers.

The main traditional activity of the Nguni tribes is cattle herding. In the old days chiefs would count their wealth by the size of their herd. Single-colored cattle were especially prized and could command high prices. The cattle provided the families with milk, which in various forms became a basic foodstuff, and could be slaughtered for meat on special occasions.

The cattle were kept in stockades of stone or tough wooden fences, being driven out to graze by the boys, who were also expected to protect the cattle against lions and leopards. Each family had a recognised area of grazing land. If they strayed beyond their grazing area trouble, perhaps warfare, could flare up.

The ideology of cattle played a large role in society. Chiefs were often referred to as bulls. In one tribe the inauguration of a new chief involved a complicated ceremony during which he sat astride a great black bull.

Other sources of food played a more minor role in the life of the Nguni, but were no less important for health. Small gardens of grain and vegetables would be grown around the kraal. It was the task of the women to tend the crops. After harvest the grain was milled by being placed in deep wooden bowls and continuously pounded with large wooden pestles which were often larger than their users. The grain was then boiled up, often

Cheetahs often spend long hours resting on termite mounds (left) keeping a careful eye on the surrounding grasslands for potential prey. Having run down a vicitm by their superior speed, cheetahs lose little time devouring the hapless antelope (far left). Above: A cheetah watches the sun set over Londolozi Game Reserve. Facing page: A white-backed vulture spreads its wings to the dying sun.

with milk, to form a stiff, heavy porridge. This was then divided into pieces and used as bread. It could be dipped into savory stews made of meat or relish, or eaten plain.

The influence of more northerly groups can be seen in the Nguni initiation ceremonies. When the boys reached maturity they went through an elaborate initiation. These ceremonies often lasted many weeks and involved painting the body with white clay and ritual washing. The boys would be instructed in the rules of society, and the penalties for transgressing them. Finally their old clothes and toys would be burnt to symbolise the abandonment of childhood.

The boys were then formed into age groups and lived together with young men from other villages. Such formations formed the fighting strength of a tribe and are generally known as regiments. Nguni society was strongly militaristic, with cattle raids and revenge killings being commonplace.

In the early 19th century this society was manipulated and transformed by a strong

Facing page: A female yellowbarb spider waits on its web for a victim to enmesh itself. Right: The foam nest frog. Below left: A praying mantis. Below: A pair of bush locusts. Bottom: A pair of scorpions about to commence their ritual courtship dance. They will lock pincers and drag each other to and fro for some time. Overleaf: Sun City, South Africa.

young warrior who stood inches taller than any other. His name was Shaka, chief of the Zulu tribe. He scorned the traditional raids in favor of pitched battles and wholesale massacre.

Shaka became chief in 1816 and at once reorganized his army. The yearly regiments were transformed by strict military discipline and new, more deadly weapons. Within two years they had exterminated the armies of two neighboring tribes. The survivors were broken up from their families and regiments and incorporated within the ranks of the Zulu.

More conquests followed swiftly, the powerful Ndwandwe tribe being crushed and added to the Zulu. By 1828 Shaka had conquered all neighboring tribes, breaking up their social structure and welding them to

The rocky cliffs of the Cape of Good Hope, the southernmost point in Africa. Below: A colony of jackass penguins. These birds thrive along the western coast of South Africa because of a cold offshore current. Right: Cape fur seals come ashore to breed on the rocky Skeleton Coast. Facing page top: A flock of ostriches. Facing page bottom: A group of Zulu men perform a traditional dance in tribal costume. Overleaf: An aerial view of Cape Town looking towards Table Mountain.

his own. His army numbered 20,000 men and was a model of discipline and efficiency. Shaka's successors, his brothers and nephews, continued to expand the Zulu Empire until it covered thousands of square miles and supported an army of 50,000 spears.

When at its height, the Zulu Empire clashed with the expanding British Cape Colony. Despite early successes, an entire British column of over 1,000 men was massacred. The Zulu were defeated in 1879 and their Empire broken up and taken into the British Empire.

It was the coming of the European influence which transformed southern Africa into the prosperous industrialised land which so much of it has become, yet the first European contacts were slight and seemed incredibly unimportant to most of the people of the southern part of the continent.

First to arrive were the Portuguese in the late 15th century. They had already found rich trading lands in West Africa and were keen to push on to fresh areas. They also cherished the hope that if they sailed far enough to the south they would round the base of Africa and have a clear sail to the

wealthy lands of India. Both these hopes were realised when, in 1488, Bartholemeo Diaz sailed his ship around the Cape of Good Hope.

At the Cape, Diaz found a fertile land, very different from the deserts of Africa's south-west coast. He also found that the coast trended away northwards. Ten years later his compatriot, Vasco da Gama, sailed around the Cape and reached India.

European ships continued to drop in on the coast of southern Africa at intervals over the following centuries to pick up fresh water, but no serious effort at settlement was made. That changed in 1652 when the Dutchman Jan van Riebeck landed in Table Bay. He had been sent by the Dutch East India Company with orders to found a settlement which would produce food to revictual ships sailing to the Dutch East Indies.

Cape Town, as the settlement became known, flourished in its little way. The Dutch did not encourage new settlers because it did not need to do so. Only about three dozen ships called each year and van Riebeck's small band of companions could provide for their wants. But the settlers came anyway, encouraged by reports of the fertility of the coastal

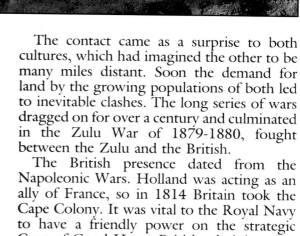

Facing page top: The Yacht Basin at Gordon's Bay, South Africa. Facing page bottom: A fine sandy beach close to Cape Town. Above right: The precipitous flanks of Table Mountain. Right: An aerial view of the Cape of Good Hope. Below right: The Old Town Hall of Cape Town, which dates from Victorian times. Overleaf: the Cape of Good Hope.

The contact came as a surprise to both cultures, which had imagined the other to be many miles distant. Soon the demand for land by the growing populations of both led to inevitable clashes. The long series of wars dragged on for over a century and culminated in the Zulu War of 1879-1880, fought between the Zulu and the British.

The British presence dated from the Napoleonic Wars. Holland was acting as an ally of France, so in 1814 Britain took the Cape Colony. It was vital to the Royal Navy to have a friendly power on the strategic Cape of Good Hope. British administration proved to be unpopular with many Boers, who moved inland taking their herds and culture with them. They founded two inland republics stretching from the Orange to the

strip.

Nor were the newcomers disappointed. The hills south of the Karoo enjoy a soft Mediterranean-style climate ideal for the growing of European-style crops. Gradually the colony spread along the coast, with settlers rapidly progressing from subsistence agriculture to the production of cash crops, such as wine and sugar.

By the mid 18th century the colonists had formed a distinct culture, with a language which was, and remains, a variant of Dutch. The Boers, as the settlers were becoming increasingly known, continued to expand. They formed a frontier culture, much as occurred in North America, based on self-sufficient families on widely scattered farms.

By this time the Boers had expanded beyond the hospitable Mediterranean style coast and were driving herds of domestic cattle and sheep across the scrubby pasture land beyond. In the 1760s the more wide-ranging Boers came across the scattered outposts of the Nguni peoples on the banks of the Great Fish River.

Limpopo.

Meanwhile British explorers, missionaries and soldiers pushed further inland, founding colonies which now form the nations of Zimbabwe, Zambia, Malawi and Botswana. German settlers extended control over modern Namibia while the Portuguese thrust inland from coastal bases to establish control over Mozambique and Angola.

Following the bitter Boer War of 1899-1902 the inland Boer republics were taken over by the British. When the German possessions passed into British hands during World War I, the picture of late colonialism in southern Africa was complete.

But even before that date the colonial map was breaking up. In 1910 the Union of South Africa gained virtual self government

South Africa is famous for its flowers. The diverse climate, ranging from Mediterranean on the coast to savannah and alpine inland, coupled with the vagaries of topography creates a wide variety of environments.

In all some 16,000 species of plant flourish in the country, of which the most spectacular are the various types of protea (these pages). Overleaf: Beaches near Cape Town.

from Britain and soon became an independent nation. During the 1960s Britain granted independence to her colonies, to be followed in 1975 by Portugal. When, in 1980, Rhodesia became Zimbabwe, the present political map of southern Africa was complete.

The oldest permanently settled city in the area is Cape Town. It is also the largest and, to many eyes, the most beautiful. Much of this is due to the city's fantastic setting. Nestled between the hills around Table Bay, the city is enclosed in a natural amphitheatre which opens out on to the glittering blue waters of the South Atlantic.

Backing the city is the massive, dominating presence of Table Mountain. This 3,000 foot high mountain extends around the inland side of the city. Its lower slopes are built up, but the precipitous upper slopes have escaped development. The rocky cliff faces and steep gradients dotted with thorn trees sweep upwards to the flat summit. On certain days a white, wispy cloud will form on the summit and come rolling down towards the city. This is the famous 'Tablecloth', and its appearance can be dazzling in the bright sun.

The extraordinary formation was created by the existence of wide beds of sedimentary rocks, the upper layers of which are harder than the lower. On Table Mountain the tough top layer remained intact, while all around the softer rocks were exposed and worn away.

A cable car takes tourists up to the top of the mountain, while souvenir merchants sell their wares along the road leading up to the cable car. On the summit most people are surprised to find that the rock is not as flat as

Facing page top: The scenic wonders of Champagne Castle. Facing page bottom: The deserted coastline north of Cape Town. Top: The sun sets over Hort Bay. Above: flowers bloom in Namaqualand. Left: A magnificent protea bloom, the national flower of South Africa. Overleaf: The coast road winds away from Cape Town.

it appears from a distance. The surface is cut by many deep fissures and gullies. More than one unwary visitor has lost his life here.

The view, however, is stunning. From Table Mountain the whole of Cape Town is laid out like a model city. The busy port and towering buildings of the city center lie in the distance, beside the ocean. Closer at hand are the homes and residential areas, some surrounded by pleasant greenery, others by concrete. It is a stupendous sight.

Cutting through the heart of Cape Town is the lower, but equally dramatic Lion Mountain. This long low ridge terminates in a tall, sheer sided pinnacle with a deep notch cut from its forward slope. In profile the mountain looks like nothing more than a lion resting with its head raised in alertness. It is this which gave the peak its name. A road takes sightseers to the summit of the lion's body for a view every bit as stunning as that from Table Mountain.

The oldest building in the city, possibly the oldest structure in sub-Saharan Africa, is the Castle of Good Hope. The fortress was built in 1666 by the Dutch to protect their

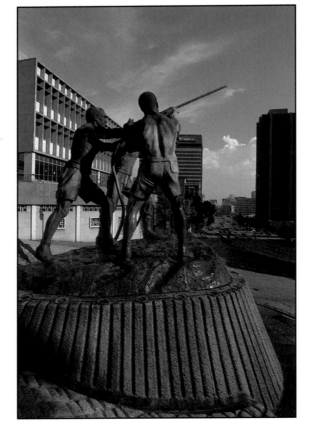

Above and facing page: The high-rise modern skyline of Johannesburg, a city which owes its existence to the vast deposits of gold ore which lie beneath the surface of the open veldt. Left: A bowls club in Johannesburg. Below: The Johannesburg mining memorial, a tribute to the thousands of men who work below ground to extract the gold. Overleaf: The Drakensberg Mountains.

settlement from raids by European fleets. For many years it served as the home of the Governor, before more comfortable quarters could be built elsewhere.

The Old Town Hall, dating from 1893, is a pleasant neo-Classical structure which fronts onto a wide square known as the Grand Parade. Normally this square is a car park for city workers, but on certain days it blossoms into a market. A wide range of goods is offered for sale, everything from cloth to leather goods and kitchen ware. Even when the market is not open smaller stalls selling flowers and fruit and vegetables can be found on the sidewalks.

Not far away is Greenmarket Square, in the oldest area of the city. The cobblestones and colonial style buildings do not date back to the 16th century, but this is the site of the oldest market in the city and is a very pleasant spot to stop for a drink.

The buildings in the old quarter of the town are a gentle reminder of the Dutch heritage of the Cape. The curling facades and tall windows, familiar to all who have visited Amsterdam, can be seen. But in Cape Town, the traditional style has been given a definite

colonial flavor with more solid lines and spreading verandas. A classic example is the Old Town House, built in 1755.

The British have also left their mark, perhaps best epitomised at the Mount Nelson Hotel. This magnificent structure is fronted by a Greek-style free-standing portico painted a brilliant white which gleams unnaturally in the sunshine.

The city's heart is a monument to neither the British nor Dutch, but to the dynamic business world of the late 20th century. High rise offices and business developments crowd the skyline, dwarfing older buildings.

The coast around Cape Town is the site of several breeding colonies of the most out of place animals. Jackass penguins, usually confined to the chilly seas around Antarctica, flourish on Marcus Island and can be found as far north as the Angolan border. The reason for this unusual distribution is the cold Benguela Current which sweeps up the western coast of southern Africa, bringing waters from deep within the Antarctic seas. The sea is, therefore, within the temperature range enjoyed by penguins.

The small birds come ashore in large groups, numbering several hundred, to breed. They congregate on the sandy beaches and waddle into the rocky interior. Here they lay their eggs, remaining with the chick for several weeks until it is old enough to take to the sea. The parents co-operate in the care of the young. While one remains at the nest to guard the chick against predators, the other puts to sea in search of food. The adult birds alternate between shore and sea for some weeks, then abandon the chick to find its own

Facing page: The clouds gather around the flanks of the high mountains behind Pretoria. This page: Vineyards and wineries around Stellenbosch and Paarl. The South African wine industry was begun by Governor de Stel nearly 300 years ago. The vineyards he founded, known as the Constantia, produced a fine strong wine which was eagerly bought by noblemen throughout Europe. Current trends are towards fresher, lighter wines. Overleaf: Swimmers and surfers off the beaches at Durban.

way in the world.

For most of the year the penguins swim the waters of the southern oceans hunting for the fish on which they feed. In their journeying they may well come across another breeding visitor to African coasts, the seal.

Some areas of the coast are thick with seals during the mating season. The large, lumbering males will ferociously defend their territory against all comers, while the females spend their time nursing their young. During the breeding season most species of seal do not feed. They live off their reserves of stored fat and blubber.

Some miles to the east of Cape Town, crouching in the Bergrivier Valley at the foot of the 4,000 foot Holland Mountains, is the town of Paarl. This quiet settlement is typical of many other farming communities in the western Cape. The low-lying buildings are surrounded by wide agricultural fields and orchards. But most important are the vineyards.

Paarl lies on virtually the same latitude as the famous wine producing regions of Spain and Portugal, though in the opposite hemisphere. The growers round Paarl almost consciously imitate their northern counterparts by producing 'sherry' and 'port'. They use the identical, traditional techniques as are used in the north and produce some very good fortified wines.

In the past twenty years the estate owners around Paarl, and the nearby Stellenbosch, have been improving their methods of producing table wines. Paarl Steen is perhaps the best white wine, for those who prefer dry wines, while those with a sweeter tooth might prefer the Riesling. Red wines also flourish around Stellenbosch, being produced from pinot noir and gamay grapes.

Today the South African wine industry is dominated by the giant company of KWV, which is centered at Paarl. It is KWV which sets the standards against which others measure themselves and who dominate the export market, most of which goes to Europe.

Stellenbosch was named in honor of Governor de Stel, the second Dutch Governor of Cape Colony. It was he who planted the first vineyards of South Africa at Constantia above False Bay. His beautiful, spreading winery still stands, though it is now the center of a farm rather than a vineyard.

The soft climate of the Cape is ideal for farming and it was this which gave Cape Colony its start. But the true prosperity of the nation lay not in agriculture, nor in the great herds which were driven north to graze on the grasslands beyond the Orange River. It lay in the mineral wealth which was hidden beneath the soil.

The most dramatic sign of the mineral wealth of South Africa can be seen at Kimberley, the heart of the diamond industry. Diamonds were first discovered here in

1871, by a farmer who noticed his son using an odd pebble in a game of marbles. The clear pebble turned out to be a diamond of outstanding quality, unfortunately nobody believed a word about it.

When the diamond reached London it was finally pronounced genuine, but still nobody wanted to take up the opportunity of investing money in a diamond mining business. The gem world had suffered several frauds and swindles in the previous few years and most thought the Kimberley find might prove to be another. One scientist scornfully asserted that if the diamond had not been planted by human hands it must have been carried there by an ostrich.

Only when other gems were found did outsiders believe the local Boer farmers' claims. Then money and miners poured into the area. Activity soon centered around a hill near Kimberley. The entire hill was quickly dug away by miners, who then began to push down into the earth. As the hole deepened the problems of shoreing up the sides became too great for individual miners. The De Beers mining company, led by Cecil Rhodes, bought out the individual miners. Large scale mining equipment was brought in and the diamond mine became a gigantic undertaking.

Before mining stopped in 1914 the company had excavated the largest hole in the world. Known locally as simply the Big Hole,

the old mine covers 35 acres and is 2,500 feet deep. Nearly 30 million tons of earth and rock were removed to create the hole, of which just 3 tons were diamonds. A museum, detailing the history of diamond mining in the area stands nearby, as does a magnificent bronze fountain which celebrates the efforts of the early diamond miners.

The new mine is a few hundred yards to the east. This is also an open cast mine and in a few years time should be even larger than the Big Hole.

If the stupendous size of the Kimberley mine is open for all to see, that of the Johannesburg gold mines is hidden. The gold mines of the Transvaal are the largest in the world. The East Rand Mine at Boksburg covers no less than 12,000 acres. Nearby, at Carletonville the Western Deep Mine plunges more than 2 miles beneath the

Above: The beautiful jacaranda trees which line the suburban roads of Pretoria. Right and top: The fine, restrained architecture of the Union Buildings which dominate Pretoria, the capital of the Union of South Africa. Facing page: A view across Pretoria from the terraced gardens of the Union Buildings. Overleaf: One of many statues in the grounds of the Union Buildings.

ground, making it the deepest in the world.

The great city of Johannesburg has grown up as a direct result of these gold mines. Centered on the Rand, a ridge of rock where the richest mines are located, the city spreads out for nearly sixty square miles and is home to more than one and a half million people. Numerous satellite towns boost the population even higher.

It is possible to book visits around the mines. The least adventurous would probably settle for a tour of the surface workings, though exhausting trips below ground are organised. The majority of visitors, though are content to visit the dramatic mine dances.

Workers at the mines come from many areas and several nations. At public displays the men perform traditional dances as part of an effort to maintain their old tribal life in the heart of a modern city. In costumes of outstanding beauty the workers perform war chants and celebratory dances which might otherwise only live in ethnologists notebooks.

Though the incredibly rich gold mines are the basis of Johannesburg they are not the only source of wealth for the city. Not many miles away are extensive coal deposits and sources of iron ore. Large steelworks and coal mines produce work and feed the industries of the area.

This is not the only sign at ground level of the mine workings. Scattered along the Rand are many strangely regular hills. These long, narrow heights are not the result of some odd geological quirk. They are the mounds made up of waste rock excavated from the mines. Several tons of rock must be extracted to get even the smallest amount of gold. The simplest answer to the disposal of the waste is to pile it up, landscape it and leave it on the surface.

Like many another industrial town, Johan-

These pages: Elephants roam the grasslands and open thorn forests in small herds. Within the herd elephants maintain a complex social organisation, however an occasional individual will leave the herd for a solitary existance. These are often males and are referred to as rogues. Some rogues are extremely bad-tempered and will attack anyone, or anything, which disturbs them. Overleaf: A large herd of Burchell's zebra.

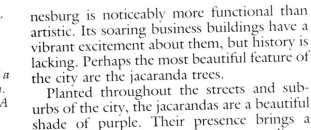

In common with other animals which live together in family groups, lions (these pages) have developed a complex social pattern. Facing page bottom: A lioness carries a one month old cub by the scruff of its neck. Below: A lioness nursing her cubs. Facing page top: A lioness with a pair of older cubs. By this age the cubs are following the pride in the hunt and may be allowed to participate in a kill. Left: A male lion with a springbok.

nesburg is noticeably more functional than artistic. Its soaring business buildings have a vibrant excitement about them, but history is lacking. Perhaps the most beautiful feature of the city are the jacaranda trees.

Planted throughout the streets and suburbs of the city, the jacarandas are a beautiful shade of purple. Their presence brings a touch of color to the city and is surroundings. The jacaranda trees are a dominant feature of the countryside north of Johannesburg, between that city and Pretoria.

Though only 30 miles distant from the center of Johannesburg, Pretoria seems a world away. Gone are the thrusting reminders of dynamic economic growth, to be replaced by quiet suburbs and broad city streets. Perhaps the difference is due to the origins of Pretoria.

While Johannesburg was begun as a tough

mining town of the 19th century, Pretoria's main purpose is to be the administrative center of the nation. It is fitting that the Union Buildings, where the South African Parliament sits, should dominate the city from their slight hill.

The buildings were built ninety years ago to the designs of Sir Herbert Baker, the British architect who went on to build many important structures. In South Africa he designed the Rhodes Memorial on Table Mountain while in England his structures include South Africa House, the Bank of England and several war memorials. He also had a hand in the construction of New Delhi as the center for the British Raj in India.

Though on a smaller scale than his later works, the Union Buildings are often considered to be Baker's finest work. The smooth, curving colonnade of the central section, flanked by a pair of domes sits easily at the top of the terraced gardens and long staircase which run down the slope towards the city. It is a building of charm and elegance.

Very different is the massive Voortrecker Monument which dominates the skyline to the south. This massive, square building stands well over 100 feet high and has a stark simplicity made all the more impressive by its sheer bulk. The monument commemorates the Great Trek, which brought the Boers

inland from the coast to the land where the inland cities now stand.

The city of Durban, on the east coast enjoys the rare distinction of being both a major port and major holiday resort. The port is linked by rail and road with the inland cities of Pietermaritzberg and Ladysmith as well as the broad hinterland of northern South Africa. Vast amounts of goods, both industrial and agricultural, come along this network for shipment abroad.

At the same time the beaches around the city are remarkably clean. The subtropical climate, Durban is warm throughout the winter, makes them amazingly popular. At any time of the year bathers can be seen lounging on the beaches or alongside the many pools of the area. The seafront is lined by large, modern hotels, which cater to the tastes of most visitors. The only drawback to this almost idyllic setting are the sharks. Most major beaches are protected by gillnets, but shark attacks do occur from time to time. It is the price to be paid for year-round warm water.

One of the most popular beach sports is shore fishing. In rough weather, several

beaches will be lined by fishermen armed with long, supple rods. Greenfish and shad are readily taken while barracuda are sometimes hauled in. Those equipped with heavier tackle will haul in sharks. More than one person, who until then has been swimming

Natal, the eastern coastal area of South Africa, has a diverse collection of wildlife. Top: A cape fox with cubs. Above left: a steinbuck. Above right: A yellow mongoose with her young. Left: A cape pangolin. Facing page bottom: A Nile crocodile, which actually ranges throughout Africa and is not restricted to the river after which it is named. Facing page top: A group of hippopotamoses wallow in a pool of liquid mud.

from nearby beaches, has been startled by the sight of a 15 foot shark being hauled ashore.

Away from the cities, ports and mines where the economic wealth of South Africa is found, the old style of life continues much as before. There are spreading farms growing cash crops on the large scale and traditional Nguni farms herding cattle and growing small amounts of maize.

In other areas even this limited economic activity has no place. The Drakensberg Mountains, inland of Durban, are wild territory characterised by rugged terrain, deep valleys and raging mountain streams. rising to over 10,000 feet, the Drakensberg have a covering of sparkling snow during the winter months. They are famed as a center for walking and camping holidays and are a considerable tourist attraction.

Perhaps more popular are the National Parks. Of these easily the most famous is the Kruger, which covers a vast area of plains in northeastern South Africa. Within the park boundaries is a wide variety of habitat, and perhaps the greatest collection of wildlife in Africa. There are the standard collection of big game, antelope, zebra and big cats, together with a huge variety of insects, reptiles and other small animals.

Rather less popular, if only because of its complete remoteness, is the Kalahari-Gemsbok. Tucked between the Nossob River and the Namibian border, this park is reached by no major road and a four wheel vehicle is essential for visitors. On the hard dry plains of Kalahari-Gemsbok can be seen the rarest of the African cats, the fleet-footed cheetah.

The continent of Africa is a place of stupendous contrasts. The game parks preserve the oldest and most spectacular face of Africa. Yet the dynamic factories which are springing up across the continent are a sign of changing times, when modern technology is coming to bring prosperity and better living conditions to the peoples of Africa.

Above all it is a continent of unrivalled beauty.

PHOTOGRAPHERS' INDEX